GREECE OLD AND NEW

Greece Old and New

Edited by
Tom Winnifrith and Penelope Murray

St. Martin's Press   New York

Library of Congress Cataloging in Publication Data

Main entry under title:

Greece old and new.

Lectures, sponsored by the Greek Embassy and presented at the University of Warwick in 1978 and 1979.
Includes index.
Contents: Invocation to the muses / by Penelope Murray — Two archaic ages of Greece / by George Forrest — Homer today / by Malcolm Willcock — [etc.]
1. Civilization, Greek—Addresses, essays, lectures. 2. Byzantine Empire—Civilization—Addresses, essays, lectures. I. Winnifrith, Tom. II. Murray, Penelope.
DF77.G77 1982   949.5   81-21232
ISBN 0-312-34716-2   AACR2

84-7060

Contents

List of Plates

Plate 4b is by courtesy of the Ashmolean Museum; plates 3b, 4a and 7b are by courtesy of the Gennadius Library; plate 6c is by courtesy of the German Archaeological Institute, Athens; plate 6b is by courtesy of the *Illustrated London News*; plates 5a, 5b, 6a, 7a, 8a and 8b are by courtesy of the Mansell Collection and plate 6d is by courtesy of Ronald Sheridan.

List of Maps and Figures

Acknowledgements

In 1978 and 1979 the Greek Embassy sponsored a series of lectures at the University of Warwick designed to show the similarities and differences between the history and literature of Ancient and Modern Greece. In publishing these lectures the editors and the University of Warwick would like to thank the Greek Embassy for their generous help, and they would also like to thank their audience for their support through fog, frost and snow, rail strikes, petrol shortages and the railway line buckled in the heat of May which nearly postponed Mr St Clair's lecture for a second time.

In putting on the lectures the Joint School of Classical Civilisation received timely help from Mr J. B. Butterworth, Vice-Chancellor of the University of Warwick, Mrs Eleni Cubitt of the Greek Embassy, the Secretary of the Oxford and Cambridge Schools Examination Board, the Headmistress of Ursuline Convent High School, Brentwood, Mrs Sylvia Seeley, Miss Janet Floyd, Miss Joan Miles, Mr Samuel Lieu, Mrs Penny Jefferson, Miss Karen Lawrence, Miss Jessica Wall, Miss Lynne Richards, Miss Eleanor Gurr, Miss Tina Moran, Miss Nicolette Garner and Miss Alison Keane.

In publishing the lectures the editors would like to thank Mrs Janet Bailey and Mrs Christine Wyman for their admirable typing, Miss Susan Caruth of Macmillan for her sympathetic help, and all contributors for their punctual submission of the printed version of their oral contributions.

It does not require a Milman Parry to detect differences between the various contributors when it comes to providing a written version of their lectures. The editors have felt it right to leave each contributor free to adopt his own particular stance, between winged words and the printed page, between the popular pamphlet and the learned article. Every μέν has its δέ. Likewise in trying to impose uniformity in proper names, always a nightmare for writers on Ancient Greece, always torn by the conflicting claims of Classical Greek correctness and Latinate popular usage, the editors have done their best to find a via media in a book complicated by the different feelings of different contributors, and by the different contributions of writers on ancient, medieval and modern Greece.

The editors would like to thank Noyes University Press for allowing us to reproduce the maps for Professor Hammond's article, and Mr Nikos Stangos for allowing us to print his translation of Ritsos's poem.

The editors and publishers wish to thank the following who have kindly given permission for the use of copyright material: Equinox (Oxford) Ltd, for the figure from *The Emergence of Greece* by A. E. Johnstone in *The Making of the Past* series, published by Phaidon Press Ltd, 1976; and Princeton University Press, for the figure from *The Stone of Athens*, © 1978 by Princeton University Press.

T.W.
P.M.

Notes on the Contributors

DR PENELOPE MURRAY is Lecturer in Classics at the University of Warwick.

PROFESSOR GEORGE FORREST is Wykeham Professor of Ancient History at the University of Oxford and is the author of *The Emergence of Greek Democracy* and *Ancient Sparta*.

PROFESSOR MALCOLM WILLCOCK is Professor of Latin at University College, London and has written a commentary on the *Iliad*.

PROFESSOR NICHOLAS HAMMOND was formerly Headmaster of Clifton College and Professor of Greek at the University of Bristol. He is well known for his *History of Greece* and has written books on Epirus and Macedonia.

DR TOM WINNIFRITH, a Senior Lecturer in the Department of English and Comparative Literary Studies at the University of Warwick, has written books on the Brontës, and has travelled extensively in the Balkans.

PROFESSOR ANTHONY BRYER is Director of Byzantine Studies at the University of Birmingham and organises annually an international symposium of Byzantine scholars. He is principally interested in the Greeks of Anatolia.

PROFESSOR ROBERT BROWNING is Professor of Classics at Birkbeck College, London; his books include *Medieval and Modern Greek*, *Justinian and Theodora* and *Byzantium and Bulgaria*.

DR PAUL CARTLEDGE is Lecturer in Ancient History at the University of Cambridge, was formerly Lecturer in Classics at the University of Warwick and is the author of *Sparta and Lakonia*.

WILLIAM ST CLAIR is the President of the Byron Society and the author of a study of philhellenes in the Greek War of Independence, *That Greece Might Still Be Free*.

NIKOS STANGOS is himself a poet, and has translated poems by Yannis Ritsos in the *Penguin Modern European Poets* series.

1 Invocation to the Muses

Penelope Murray

The Greeks have taught us that at the beginning of every task the poet should invoke the Muses; and, unfashionable as such appeals may be, they surely have their place in any investigation of the relation between Greece old and new. It is precisely the continuing significance of the invocation, and especially its meaning to the poet, that I wish to discuss.

In its oldest forms, the belief in poetic inspiration seems to have been genuinely religious: this religious feeling can have various manifestations, but in particular the work of the Chadwicks has shown that a leading figure in many primitive societies, both ancient and modern, is the seer. The seer combines the functions of poet, prophet and philosopher: he has the gifts of poetry and of special knowledge, both of which are believed to be the result of divine inspiration. Even where the various functions of the seer are seen as separate, the analogy between the poet and the prophet can be closely felt. This was certainly the case in early Greek poetry, whether or not the concept of the seer itself is applicable to Ancient Greece. Pindar, for example, saw himself as a chosen being, an intermediary between gods and men, the 'prophet of the Muses' (*Paean*, 6.6). Hesiod described how the Muses called him to be a poet whilst he was tending his sheep on Mount Helicon:

And once they taught Hesiod fair song, when he was tending his sheep at the foot of sacred Helicon. These were the words which the goddesses first spoke to me — the Olympian Muses, daughters of Zeus the aegis-bearer: 'Shepherds dwelling in the fields, shameful wretches, nothing but bellies, we know how to speak

1

many false things as though they were true; but we know when we wish, how to utter true things.' So spoke the daughters of great Zeus, ready of speech. And they plucked a branch of flourishing laurel and gave it to me as a staff, a wonderful thing, and they breathed into me a divine voice so that I might celebrate the events of the future and of the past. They bade me sing of the race of the blessed eternal gods, but always to sing of themselves first and last.

                                              (*Theogony*, 22–34)

This description closely resembles the prophet Amos' account of his religious calling:

I was no prophet, neither was I a prophet's son; but I was an herdsman, and a gatherer of sycamore fruit: and the Lord took me as I followed the flock, and the Lord said unto me, Go, prophesy unto my people Israel.

                                              (*Amos*, 7.14–15)

Similarly the Venerable Bede records how the Anglo-Saxon religious poet, Caedmon, received the gift of divine inspiration from an angel whilst he was tending his cows. The poet's vocation, no less than the prophet's, can be described in genuinely religious terms. Moreover there are still poets in certain societies today who regard their gifts in a similar way. For example, Radlov quotes the words of a Kara–Kirghiz bard:

I can sing every song; for God has planted the gift of song in my heart. He gives me the word on my tongue without my having to seek it. I have learned none of my songs. All springs up from my inner being and goes forth from it.

Whether or not all concepts of poetic inspiration originally had this religious significance, the idea of poetic inspiration persists even after it has lost its religious force in order to account for the belief of many poets (and indeed non-poets) that the creation of poetry depends at least in part on something beyond man's control. The experience which gives rise to the concept of poetic inspiration has been described by many poets at different periods. Obviously this experience will vary from poet to poet, but an essential feature of it is the feeling that poetry comes from some source other than the conscious mind; and the similarities between the numerous descriptions of inspiration that we have suggest that they relate to an experience which is essentially the same within different cultures and different ages. What varies is the interpretation of such experiences rather than the experiences themselves. Broadly speaking, allowing for certain exceptions, there has been a progression from religious to secular interpretations. Primitive peoples believe that the seer-poet's inspiration derives from contact with super-natural powers; similarly the Greeks attributed poetic inspiration to the Muses, Christian writers to the Holy Spirit. The religious interpretation of inspiration was predominant throughout the Renaissance until the seventeenth century.

In the Neoclassical period the whole concept of poetic inspiration was challenged fundamentally, and several critics repudiated inspiration as the source of poetry altogether. For example, Thomas Hobbes, in his *Answer to Davenant's Preface to Gondibert* (1650), welcomed Davenant's attack on the concept of poetic inspiration, saying:

But why a Christian should think it an ornament to his poem, either to profane the true God or invoke a false one, I can imagine no cause but of reasonless imitation of custom, of a foolish custom, by which a man enabled to speak wisely from the principles of nature and his own meditation, loves rather to be thought to speak by inspiration, like a bagpipe.

Those critics who accepted the fact of poetic inspiration preferred to regard it as a natural rather than a supernatural phenomenon. Alexander Gerard, for example, explained inspiration in terms of the mechanical workings of the mind:

When an ingenious track of thinking presents itself, though but casually, to the genius, occupied it may be with something else, imagination darts alongst it with great rapidity; and by this rapidity its ardour is more inflamed. The velocity of its motion sets it on fire like a chariot wheel which is kindled by the quickness of its revolution. . . . Its motions become still more impetuous, till the mind is enraptured with the subject, and exalted into an ecstasy. In this manner the fire of genius, like a divine impulse, raises the mind above itself, and by the natural influence of imagination actuates it as if it were supernaturally inspired.

(*Essay on Genius*, 1774)

Edward Young, in his famous *Conjectures on Original Composition* (1759), gave a different and much more far-reaching explanation of inspiration, attributing it to the workings of the unconscious mind of genius, which he illustrated by the analogy of the spontaneous growth of plants. Young's idea of poetry springing up, plant-like, from the hidden depths of the mind had an enormous influence on the German writers of the later eighteenth century, and subsequently on the English Romantic movement.

With the advent of psychology it has become commonplace to explain the experience of inspiration in terms of the activity of the sub-conscious; in fact inspiration has been defined as the traditional name for the unconscious factor in creation. Certainly explanations of inspiration in terms of the unconscious activity of the mind appeal to those who wish to combine religious scepticism with 'scientific' accuracy. Thus in his book *The Act of Creation* (1964), Arthur Koestler argues that scientific discovery, no less than artistic creation, depends on non-rational mental processes involving sudden inspirations and flashes of insight. Inspiration occurs when rational thinking is suspended and the sub-conscious is allowed free play as, for example, in sleep and in mental illness. Koestler defines the essence of poetic creativity as 'the capacity to regress, more or less at will, to the games of the underground [the sub-conscious], without losing contact with the surface'. This may seem a far cry from the ancient interpretation of inspiration in terms of the Muses. But it illustrates the fact that despite attempts to explain the act of creation scientifically, the creative process remains as mysterious to us as it was to the Greeks.

How the idea of the Muses originated is obscure, but these goddesses appear to have been invented by the Greeks. Even the etymology of the word μοῦσα is disputed. According to one theory the word comes from the same root as the Latin word *mons* (mountain), and therefore implies that the Muses were originally mountain nymphs; but despite the undoubtedly close connections which exist between Muses and mountains on the one hand, and between Muses and nymphs on the other, this theory has not been generally accepted. There is more support amongst scholars for the derivation of μοῦσα from an original root to which are related words like μνάομαι (I am mindful of, remember) and μιμνήσκομαι (I remind). The Muses would then be 'those who are mindful' in the intransitive sense or 'those who remind' in the transitive sense. These two senses are not, of course, mutually exclusive, as we can see, for example, from the detailed invocation to the Muses before the catalogue of ships in the *Iliad*, which I shall discuss below. Vergil recalls this passage in a line which plays on the double function of the Muses as those who remember and those who remind, as well as on the function of poetry to commemorate, 'et meministis enim, divae, et memorare potestis' (*Aeneid*, 7.645). Another possibility is that μοῦσα is closely related to the word μένος (force, power or spirit) so that the Muses are givers of power. Although the precise details of the word's etymology are disputed, the majority of scholars appear to agree that μοῦσα is related to words connected with the spiritual or intellectual spheres.

But, interesting as the question of the Muses' origin is, it does not tell us very much about what they meant for the early Greek poets; if we wish to understand their significance for these poets we must investigate their function in early Greek poetry. It is clear from Homer onwards that one of the chief functions of the Muses is to sing and dance at festivities of the Olympian gods, as, for example, in the famous passage at the end of *Iliad*, Book 1, where the Muses, led by Apollo, sing for the entertainment of the gods as they feast the whole day long. The fullest and most vivid description of the Muses' activities which we have is given by Hesiod in his hymn to the Muses at the beginning of the *Theogony*: the hymn describes some of their characteristic activities — they sing and dance for their own enjoyment on Mount Helicon 'on soft feet by the dark blue water of the spring' as well as delighting the heart of their father Zeus with their harmonious voices — and includes an account of their birth from Mnemosyne (Memory):

> she bore her nine daughters, concordant
>   of heart, and singing
> is all the thought that is in them,
>   and no care troubles their spirits.
> She bore them a little way off
>   from the highest snowy summit
> of Olympus; there are their shining
>   dancing places, their handsome

houses, and the Graces and Desire live there
   beside them
in festivity; lovely is the voice
   that issues from their lips
as they sing of all the laws and all
   the gracious customs
of the immortals, and glorify them
   with their sweet voices.

                            (*Theogony*, 60–7, trans. R. Lattimore)

Hesiod's account of the birth and parentage of the Muses became
the standard one in Antiquity, although evidence from later
authors suggests that an alternative genealogy existed. Diodorus
Siculus (4.7.1.) states that some of the early poets including
Alcman made the Muses the daughters of Uranos (Heaven) and
Gaia (Earth), whilst Pausanias (9.29.4.) says that Mimnermus referred to two generations of Muses, the older the daughters of
Uranos and Gaia, the younger the daughters of Zeus. Nevertheless
it was Hesiod's genealogy which prevailed. It was also Hesiod who
first gave the Muses their familiar names: Clio, Euterpe, Thaleia,
Melpomene, Terpsichore, Erato, Polymnia, Urania and Calliope;
but it was not until much later in Hellenistic and Roman times
that the individual Muses came to be clearly differentiated according to function. Hesiod's names, which he may well have invented
himself, present a composite picture of the various activities
associated with the Muses — poetry, song, dance, instrumental
music — and also reflect their characteristic role as bringers of
praise, celebration and delight. In fact it is clear that to both
Homer and Hesiod the Muses symbolise not only the aspects of
memory and information, but even more prominently the elements of pleasure and beauty which are essential characteristics of
poetry for us as much as for the Greeks.

   The Muses' function *vis-à-vis* the gods is fairly clear, but the
same cannot be said of their dealings with men; in particular their
relationship to the poetic process is obscure. I take it as self evident
that the Muses represent in some sense the belief that poetry comes
from a source external to the poet and that this belief corresponds
in certain ways to subsequent notions of poetic inspiration. But
what exactly do the Muses do, and how do the poets conceive of
their inspiration? In considering these questions we should be
aware of the great difference between the nature of the evidence

which we have for ancient and modern notions of poetic inspiration. The Romantics and their successors not only discuss the concept in their poetry and criticism, but also record and analyse their own experiences of inspiration in letters, diaries and note-books. But the only evidence that we have for the idea of poetic inspiration in Greece, at any rate before the fifth century, is in the poetry itself. And secondly, as has often been remarked, ancient poets were not concerned with self-relevation in the way that their modern counterparts are. When ancient poets talk about themselves and their art, they are more intent on establishing their authority as poets than on arousing interest in themselves and the way they create. In fact the ancient poets tell us nothing specific about the genesis of their poetry, or their methods of composition. Nevertheless it is evident that the belief in inspiration was of central importance in their conception of poetry, and this is why the Muses play such an important part in the literature of early Greece.

Invocations to the Muses are, of course, a standard feature of early Greek poetry. In Book 2 of the *Iliad* the poet invokes the Muses before he embarks on the catalogue of ships:

> Tell me now, you Muses who have your homes on Olympus.
> For you, who are goddesses, are there, and you know all things,
> and we have heard only the rumour of it and know nothing.
> Who then of those were the chief men and the lords of the
>   Danaans?
> I could not tell over the multitude of them nor name them,
> not if I had ten tongues and ten mouths, not if I had
> a voice never to be broken and a heart of bronze within me,
> not unless the Muses of Olympia, daughters
> of Zeus of the aegis, remembered all those who came beneath
>   Ilion.
> I will tell the lords of the ships, and the ships' numbers.
>
> (*Iliad*, 2.484–93, trans. R. Lattimore)

The first thing that one notices about this invocation is that it is essentially a request for information. Although Homer does not call the Muses the daughters of Mnemosyne, a connection between memory and the Muses is strongly implied in this passage: the Muses know everything and can communicate their knowledge to the poet, who in turn commemorates the glorious deeds of the past in song. The contrast drawn in these lines between the divine knowledge of the Muses and the mortal ignorance of the poet is a recurrent theme in early Greek poetry, as is the belief that the Muses can bestow special knowledge on their chosen spokesmen. This belief is apparent not only from appeals such as the one quoted above, but also from the references to the poet as θεράπων (attendant) or ἄγγελος (messenger) of the Muses, which we find, for example, in the poetry of Hesiod, Sappho, Theognis, Bacchylides and Pindar. The idea of the poet as a special being who, through his relationship with the Muses, has access to knowledge hidden from ordinary mortals is particularly prominent in Pindar, as can be seen from his proud claim in *fragment*, 70b. 23–5: 'The Muse has raised me up as a chosen herald of wise words for Greece', or from his description of himself as the 'prophet of the Muses'. Like the bard in the *Iliad*, but with more awareness of his own special nature, Pindar speaks with the authority which comes from divine revelation:

> The gods can persuade the wise of these things, but it is impossible for mortals to discover them. But since you, maiden Muses, know everything – you have had this allotted to you with the cloud-wrapped father and Mnemosyne – listen now.
>
> *(Paean*, 6.51–8)

This association of the Muses with knowledge does not correspond to modern notions of poetic inspiration, but the widespread occurrence of it in early Greek poetry suggests that inspiration and knowledge were closely linked during this period. In fact the conviction that the poet's claim to knowledge is spurious is at the heart of Plato's attack on poetry. Plato's attitude to poetry is, of course, ambivalent, ranging from the banishing of poets from his ideal state in the *Republic* to his eulogy of them in dialogues such as the *Ion* ('a poet is a light creature, winged and holy') and the *Phaedrus*. But the one point on which Plato insists throughout his writings is that, however beautiful the products of poetic inspiration may be, poets have no knowledge of what they do; as Socrates says in the *Apology*:

> I soon realised that the poets did not compose their poems through wisdom, but by nature, and that they were inspired like seers and soothsayers: these people too say many beautiful things, but they understand nothing of what they say.
>
> *(Apology*, 22 B–C.)

This notion that the poetic process is largely intuitive and cannot be rationally explained was to become one of the central tenets of

Romantic critical theory, and indeed is still widely held today. Thomas Carlyle offers us a description of poetic inspiration which is essentially the same as Plato's, although expressed in a more extreme form:

> Manufacture is intelligible, but trivial; Creation is great, but cannot be understood. Thus if the Debater and Demonstrator, whom we may rank as the lowest of true thinkers, knows what he has done, and how he did it, the Artist, whom we may rank as the highest, knows not; must speak of Inspiration, and in one or the other dialect, call his work the gift of a divinity.
>
> (*Characteristics*, 1831)

The one vital difference between Plato and his Romantic successors is that the Romantics valued poetry and poets for precisely the reason that Plato derided them.

But to return to early Greek poetry, what do the Muses do apart from bestowing knowledge on bards? Sometimes the poet simply asks the goddesses to help him begin, suggesting that they provide the immediate impulse to song. This idea is clearly expressed in the description of Demodocus at *Odyssey*, 8.73: 'The Muse moved the bard to sing of the glorious deeds of men.' On other occasions the Muses, who are themselves traditionally sweet-voiced, are invoked to lend charm and sweetness to the poet's song, qualities which are especially important in poetry composed for performance as all early Greek poetry was. The connection between the Muses' inspiration and performance is particularly clear in Pindar's request at the beginning of *Nemean*, 3:

> Lady Muse, our mother, I beg you,
> Come in the holy Nemean month
> To Aegina's welcoming Dorian island.
> By Asopos' water young men are waiting,
> Craftsmen of honey-toned songs, in desire of your voice.
>
> (trans. C. M. Bowra)

Similarly the chorus in Aristophanes' *Acharnians* call on the Muse to give appropriate sparkle to their performance:

> Come hither, glowing charcoal Muse,
> With fiery power thy friends infuse.
> . . . send thy gleam

To us the members of thy deme,
That we may sing in concord fair
A proud melodious country air.

(665–75, trans. A. H. Sommerstein)

It is interesting to see that even in this relatively early period there is a tendency to stress different aspects of the Muses' inspiration in different genres of poetry. Epic poets invoke the Muses to give them information, and this convention persists throughout ancient literature, as we can see from, for example, the invocations in Vergil's *Aeneid*. Similarly poets like Pindar, who are writing for public occasions, claim to have knowledge from the Muses in order to stress the seriousness of their poetry and to guarantee the truth of their message. On the other hand some of the monodic lyric poets, Sappho for example, whose poetry is of a more personal nature, are less concerned to tell the truth than to give pleasure. Their invocations to the Muses seem to be more often for sweetness than for knowledge. And Aristophanes, in the context of the dramatic competition, makes his choruses invoke the Muses' aid in performance.

That the early Greek poets genuinely believed in the Muses they invoke seems to me certain. It is sometimes argued that, as the poet's self-awareness increases, so the belief in the Muses as an external source of inspiration wanes, and there is indeed a certain truth in this view. We have only to compare the opening words of the *Iliad* ('Sing, goddess, the anger of Peleus' son Achilleus') with those of the *Aeneid* ('Arms, and the man *I* sing') to see that, whereas Homer places the Muse firmly at the beginning of his poem, Vergil puts himself first, relegating the Muse to second place; it is not until line eight that he calls on the goddess to remind him of the causes of Aeneas' suffering. But self-awareness does not necessarily involve a loss of belief in the Muses. Hesiod is more self conscious, more aware of his own special nature as a poet than the Homeric bard, but the genuineness of his account of his calling (quoted above) can scarcely be doubted. Of all the early Greek poets Pindar is perhaps the most self conscious, and he certainly stresses his own part in poetic composition:

To please Tyndareos' sons, the friend of strangers,
And lovely-haired Helen is my prayer,
And to honour famous Akragas,

While I set up for Theron
An Olympian victory-song, the choicest honour
For his horses whose hooves never weary.
For this the Muse has taken her stand at my side,
And I have found a new and glittering way
To fit to a Dorian sandal the voice
Of the choir's praises.

(Olympian, 3.1–6, trans. C. M. Bowra)

Compare *Nemean* 3 in which Pindar begs the Muse to grant song from his skill, or *Nemean* 4 where he speaks of the Graces, who here take the place of the Muses, drawing forth poetry from the depths of the mind. Although Pindar places an increasing emphasis on his own poetic powers, his belief in the Muses as the source of his creativity does not seem to me to be diminished. Like all the greatest Greek poets he remains painfully conscious of the great divide between gods and men and of the transience of human existence; whatever power he has to transcend mortality through his gift of song comes from the gods:

For the gods give all the means of mortal greatness.
They grant men skill,
Might of hand and eloquence.

(Pythian, 1.42–3, trans. C. M. Bowra)

The progress of the Muses' decline ('the history of a fading metaphor') has often been charted, from Aristophanes' caricature of Euripides' Muse as a dancing girl with castanets (*Frogs* 3101–8) to the ultimate rejection of the Muses and their inspiration in Persius:

I have never wet my lips at Hippocrene's fountain, nor do I remember having any dream on twin-peaked Parnassus, so that I might suddenly come forth a poet. I leave the Muses and the pallid fountain of Pirene to those whose statues the pliant ivy caresses.

(Prologue, 1–6)

But the Muses were not dead. European poets continued to invoke them, in imitation of the ancients, of course; more important, it was still possible to use the Muse as a symbol of poetic inspiration in a meaningful way. So Milton bids the Heavenly Muse:

> . . . what in me is dark
> Illumine, what is low raise and support;
> That to the height of this great argument
> I may assert Eternal Providence,
> and justify the ways of God to men.
>
> (*Paradise Lost*, 1.22–6)

and speaks of his

> . . . celestial patroness, who deigns
> Her nightly visitation unimplored,
> And dictates to me slumbering, or inspires
> Easy my unpremeditated verse.
>
> (Ibid., 9.21–4)

These expressions, far from being the conventional literary clichés they are sometimes taken to be, seem to me to represent a genuine attempt to communicate the poet's experience of inspiration through the figure of the Muse, source of the poet's creativity. It was the Greeks who gave to the western world this first symbol of poetic inspiration, whose ambiguity and ability to express different aspects of the central truth explains its importance to the poet. And still today the Muse has her worshippers. Against mechanistic psychological theories of poetic creation Robert Graves declares:

> 'What is the use or function of poetry nowadays?' is a question not the less poignant for being defiantly asked by so many stupid people or apologetically answered by so many silly people. The function of poetry is religious invocation of the Muse; its use is the experience of mixed exultation and horror that her presence excites.
>
> (*The White Goddess*, 1946)

2 Two Archaic Ages of Greece

George Forrest

It must be made quite clear at the outset that I have nothing new to say about either of these 'Two Archaic Ages of Greece', one ancient, from the eighth century B.C. to about 500 B.C., the other modern from the War of Independence to the present day. Rather, the purpose is to suggest that if we regard the latter as archaic rather than Classical we may arrive, we or others more learned than ourselves, at some new appreciation of it. Much time has been wasted by students of Modern Greece either in assuming or in rebutting an assumption which has little to do with the case; much time wasted, and some distortion introduced. To put it very crudely, these students of Modern Greece tend to fall into two classes. On the one hand there are the 'philhellenes', those who think that Greece really is, or at any rate ought to be, like Periclean Athens; fountain of the arts and cradle of democracy. But the trouble about philhellenes is that they have never much liked Greeks, not real Greeks. They worship them as once they were, or how in the misty future they might become, given proper instruction by philhellenes, but not as they are. It's all so different from the home life of our dear darling Pericles. So Alexander the Great showed his love of Pindar by destroying every other house in Thebes except his. So Titus Quinctius Flamininus announced that all Greeks should be free, but had to take severe action against quite a few Greeks who did not share his view of what constituted freedom. Later practitioners of the doctrine have been no more or less successful.

On the other side, there are the 'realists', those who like to think that they are looking at the facts full in the face and who then, with varying degrees of violence, shudder at what they see. Greeks today have nothing, but nothing, in common with their ancestors; we must take them for what they are.

It would be very wrong to mock either of these two positions. They have been taken by very learned and very splendid men. No one who heard Sir Maurice Bowra's speech to celebrate the hundred and fiftieth anniversary of Greek independence, no one who has read J. K. Campbell and P. A. O. Sherrard's brilliant book, *Modern Greece*, could deny that he has learned a lot. Yet even these works of genius, and Bowra's speech in particular was a performance of genius, missed something, and it is that 'something' that merits attention. This is trivial as a contribution to scholarship, but it is something that can make a great difference to our appreciation of the Greece we love.

Greece in 1980 is not the same as it was in, let us say, 800 B.C. It is not the same linguistically, geographically, ethnically, economically, politically. But how great is the change? The geography is not all that different, so long as we are prepared to forget the Μεγάλη ιδέα, the 'Great Idea', and that is easy enough to forget. Who in his senses would want to own Taranto? Linguistically? The first word of Modern Greek I saw was in Omonoia Square in 1947. It was Στάσις, set up on a post from which ran the bus for the British School of Archaeology. It was disturbing to ask how any language could have got itself into such an etiolated mess. How could στάσις, 'civil strife', have become a bus-stop? When fifty others joined in waiting for the same bus the answer was clear — στάσις was στάσις. In any case, no other language that I have any acquaintance with (except perhaps Romanian) has stayed so generally recognisable over such a period, and this is true of Demotiki as much as of Katharevousa.

The best introduction to Modern Greek conversation is not the latest phrase-book. It is Plato. Μάλιστα, αλήθεια, and so on. And if Plato is the best introduction to the way the Greeks talk, Greek pots are the best introduction to the way they look. Sit on the quayside in Chios or Samos, sit at a café in Thebes or even in Livadia and look at the faces. They come straight from sixth century vases. I make no anthropological, no sociological point, only the assertion; they are the same. In some mysterious way, Greece and Greekness have imposed themselves on the supposedly racially corrupt, decadent human beings who now inhabit the peninsula. The Greek people and the Greek landscape have absorbed the newcomers. Indeed, it is Greeks themselves who have always been the colonisers, the infiltrators. Consider the way they took over the Roman Empire. Consider the way they took over Byzantium and the power they contrived to keep even after the fall of Byzantium in 1453. Passing over their role in Alexandria, in British India or in the Belgian Congo, let us not forget that not many years ago one of them even appeared in a leading, if not totally reputable, role in the higher reaches of the American administration. Even Greeks are sometimes afraid of their own influence. When Rhodes was being restored to Greece after the war the Rhodians devised a delightful history of their islands. It ran: the Romans came, they went; the Arabs came, they went; the Franks came, they went; . . . the Italians came, they went; the Greeks are coming, we're leaving. But that is all by the way.

If we feel that Greeks are something like what Greeks always were, a substantial dimension of colour is added to the argument. If we feel that they are not, the comparison between these two periods of history remains interesting.

The differences of course are enormous. The involvement of Greece with foreign powers was always, I suspect, much greater than our Greek sources suggest. Relations with Phrygia or Assyria in the eighth century, which probably prompted, or at least helped to prompt, a major domestic war, relations with Lydia in the seventh and sixth, with Persia thereafter, were far more intimate and bulked far larger in Greek thinking than we are disposed to believe, and controlled many more Greek decisions than we like to think or than Greeks liked to admit. But the influence was not of the same order as has applied since the War of Independence, when Russia, France, Britain and America have, in turn or together, tried to use Greece for their own private purposes, with scant regard for Greeks or Greek interests.

Again, the Greeks of the first archaic age were on their own. It was up to them to invent mathematics, physics, metaphysics, political science and all the rest, with no outside examples to which they could turn. Today, at the very least they can look to their own past, or if they look outside they can find plenty of people prepared to tell them what they ought to do. Then they could be, they had to be, intellectual buccaneers; now they are prisoners, in part unhappily prisoners of their own past.

Still, the similarities remain. First there is economic development and consequent urban growth. In the late eighth century,
that churlish old yokel, Hesiod, was subsisting on his miserable
acres at Ascra in Boeotia, noted only, we are told by Athenaeus,
for its beetroot. And while I yield to none in my love for beetroot, I
should not like to subsist on it. By the fifth century, Hesiod's
brother was making profitable pots, digging profitable silver, sail-
ing profitable ships. Even more significantly, many other Hesiods
were producing wine, not beetroot wine, and olive oil which could
be sold on an international market. This is a point which historians
often miss. The economy of ancient Greece was always based on
agriculture, but there is a world of difference between the self-
sufficiency or local barter on which a Hesiod depended, and the
international exchange which was the mark of Classical Greece, an
international exchange which brought with it the growth of
services, shipping, banking and the like. Similarly today, something towards half the population of Greece is still employed in
agriculture or in service activities associated with agriculture.
There are obvious problems of definition here (for example, are
employees of the Agricultural Bank employed in agriculture or
not?), but the estimate is not absurdly wrong. Nevertheless the
tobacco, the peaches, the oranges, that find themselves in TIR
lorries hurtling through Yugoslavia mean a great deal more to
Greece, and a different kind of thing to Greece, than the odd ship-
load of currants that may have reached the London market in
1820. Again, these lorries are greased by, filled up with petrol by,
garaged by, men who live in Athens, or Salonika, or Patras, or
wherever cities have grown. The population of Athens in 1833
when it became the capital of Greece was something less than
5000. Now it is, shall we say, a couple of million. Again the
population of Athens in 800 B.C. could be numbered in hundreds
rather than thousands. By 500 B.C. something like a third of
humanity in Attica lived within a mile or two of the Acropolis. Say
50,000 souls. It is not the same, but it is the same kind of thing.

My main concern however, is not with economics, or with the
kind of problem that faced Hippodamus of Miletus or Professor
Doxiadis. Nor is it with the emigration which has gone on simultaneously in both cases. Then, they went as colonisers in foreign
lands, mercenaries in the service of foreign kings or as sailors or
traders. Now, they are absorbed far more into the communities in
which they settle. But, nevertheless, they are contributing directly

or indirectly to development back home, as they did before. Still, our concern is not with that; it is with the social and political consequences of all this growth.

The most important contribution the Greeks made to civilised political life was the invention of the idea that the citizen, as a member of a society, by definition had the same rights, the same duties, as other members of the society. The rights and duties were established and guaranteed not by the goodwill of any one man or group of men, but by a set of impersonal rules, the Laws of State, or, as we should put it, the Constitution. This idea was not confined to what the Greeks called democracies. It is vital to remember that. Indeed it was first put across in a serious way in Sparta, that model of oligarchic propriety. Where democracy differed from oligarchy was either in the definition of those it admitted to membership of the community (was there, for example, a property qualification?), or in the range of rights and duties it accorded its members, or both. But in each case the principle was the same: no king, no tyrant, no group of aristocrats could override the constitution, even in a state like Sparta, which retained both kings and an aristocracy. That at least was the theory; I am not saying for a moment that it worked perfectly in practice. In Athens, the application of the principle went hand-in-hand throughout with the development of her democracy. First introduced by Solon in 594 B.C., fully built into the working of the community by Cleisthenes in 508 B.C., later to be explicitly recognised and applied right across the map by Ephialtes in 462 B.C. To an Athenian of about 500 B.C., it was as fresh, as precious and as precarious as, say, the Health Service is to us. Cleisthenes was 'just the other day'. Solon was 'my grandfather told me'. It is very easy to smile in a superior kind of way at an American's neurotic response to the catch-phrase 'Law and Order', easy to be puzzled by a Russian's obsession with security, with saving the Revolution. But it must be remembered, Americans were still establishing law and order in 'grandfather's day', Russians had their revolution and saw it threatened 'when I was a boy'. Things like this are fragile, very fragile. It is no wonder that an Athenian of around 500 B.C. was very touchy about his constitution and about his democracy, about his freedom. No wonder that an Athenian democrat, particularly after Ephialtes in 462 B.C., was a conservative, in the sense that what he wanted above all else was stability. Look at, and try to understand, the astonishing remark made by a leading Athenian politician in 427 B.C. 'A state', he said, 'which has bad laws that are stable is better off than a state which has good laws which are always being changed.'

But hand-in-hand with the development of the idea of the citizen and reverence for the Constitution, went something else. I am tempted to call it the idea of class, but that would be misleading. The trouble is that there is no better word. My grandfather was a coal miner of very radical views who dug his coal beside, and sometimes underneath, the walls of a Scottish baronial hall. Extreme Socialist though he was, nothing could persuade him completely to disregard the authority of the Laird, and angel though he was, nothing could persuade him to treat his own children or grandchildren as other than obedient servants. He looked upwards, he looked downwards, he could not look sideways at others of his same calling, or same class. Now I too am a working man of, I hope, radical views, no more radical than his, yet I could not even begin to accept the authority of any Laird, and I do not impose myself too much on my children. We have lived, he and I, in different worlds.

There is, of course, an element of class awareness even in the most vertically structured aristocratic family society. There is an element of family organisation in politics, even in the most class-conscious society. Prosopographical study of the upper reaches of the Labour Party is not without its interest. But there is room for a great shift of emphasis, and a fair part of that shift had taken place in Athens by the time of the Persian Wars, though much more was to take place later. The words they used betray it. Around 600 B.C. a poor Athenian was a *Thēs*, a member of someone's household, a *Pelatēs*, someone's client, or a *Hektemoros*, a man who paid a sixth of his annual produce not to the State as a tax, but to some individual richer than himself. By about 500 B.C., *Pelatai* and *Hektemoroi* had vanished or virtually vanished, while *Thētes* were significant not as poor individuals, but as members of the whole Athenian lowest class. Hand-in-hand went a change in the composition of Athenian government. Here the most striking single constitutional act was the opening of high political office by Solon in 594 B.C. to something like double the number who had been eligible before. Double the number. Just pause and contemplate the implications of that. Has the potential governing class of Britain changed by that amount over a period of fifty years? I think the answer is 'no'. The implications are theoretical, for unfortunately there is no evidence to let us judge just how quickly or how effectively the new opportunities could be exploited. My guess is that the answer is that they were exploited pretty slowly, and certainly Athenian politics were still being managed by a fairly narrow élite well down into the fifth century. And even if the composition was gradually changing, the change is obscured not only by our ignorance of names and origins, but also by the fact that the newcomers to the élite seem merely to have taken over the tools and methods of those who were already there.

In the sixth century, and no doubt before, the word for a political ally was *Hetairos*, a comrade. But a comrade was not a man who carried the same-coloured membership card; he was someone who came to dinner to fix the next day's in-fighting. In the fifth century there were still *Hetairoi*, but they do seem to have had rather more professionalism and more organisation about them. For most other Greek states lack of evidence imposes silence, or at least forbids any attempt at a continuous story. Even with Sparta, the secrecy with which she surrounded herself, and the façade of conservative stability which she put up for other Greeks to admire (and which she managed to persuade quite a lot of them to admire) camouflaged the detail. Yet there too the same kind of thing was going on. Let me say again, it was in Sparta that the first declaration of citizens' rights was made, and the word which Spartans chose to describe their new condition is revealing. Henceforth they were to be called *Homoioi*, equals. That word shouts out an idea of class. Within that circle of *Homoioi*, kings and members of the *Gerousia*, the aristocratic council, stood out as an élite. But under them, in Sparta too, there are some traces of political mobility among the *Homoioi*, faint, it must be admitted, though those traces are.

The chief executive magistrates of Sparta, the ephors, who in origin must have been as aristocratic as the rest, are described by Aristotle in the fourth century as being conceivably of fairly common stock, and that indicates something. This is not the place to explore exactly what. But most importantly it was a Spartan, and a king at that, who made the finest statement of that principle of constitutional government with which I began. King Demaratus to King Xerxes on the eve of the Persian War:

Want has always been our neighbour in Greece, but we have courage as an ally, the courage fashioned out of wisdom and firm laws. With its help we fight off both want and slavery. When the Spartans fight singly they fight as bravely as any men, but when they fight together they are supreme among all. For though they are free men, they are not free in all respects. Law is the master whom they fear more than your subjects fear you [Xerxes]. They do what the law commands, and its command is always the same, not to flee in battle whatever the number of the enemy, but to stand and win, or die.

I should like to suggest that in spite of the peculiarities mentioned above, the complications of foreign meddling, some of it high-minded some of it not, the wars and other catastrophes, some of them brought on Greece by itself, some of them not, and in spite of other things as well, it is possible to detect traces of development on these three fronts today.

The Greek establishment is remarkably narrow and exclusive, almost as much so as the famous Hundred Families of ancient Lokris, who had the doubtful privilege of sending some of their female offspring to do temple-service in Troy. Modern Greeks have, on the whole, preferred salon-service in Paris, but the principle is the same.

An elderly aristocratic lady was knitting after breakfast on 21 April 1967 when news broke of the military coup. 'Who', she asked, 'are our dictators?' 'X, Y and Z' was the answer. A second's pause and she resumed her knitting. 'Never heard of any of them. They won't last'. This aristocracy, this establishment, was created by the War of Independence, and was quite as much then an amalgam of disparate and disagreeing factions as was the new potential Athenian élite produced by Solon in 594 B.C. They were expatriates of really distinguished lineage who returned from Russia, Constantinople and elsewhere; other expatriates of less noble birth, but sometimes greater wealth; wild and woolly chiefs from the mountains, brigands or representatives of the Turkish government or gallant freedom fighters, as fancy took them — and others. The first Prime Minister, Kapodistrias, said of the whole farrago: 'The primates are Christian Turks, the military men robbers, the men of letters fools, and the Phanariots Children of Satan.' But soon this job-lot settled down. Differences were forgotten, not quite forgotten, but papered over well enough to produce that glittering Athenian society of a hundred years ago. Then the sons of brigands went to the opera, preferably *Il Trovatore*, or *I Masnadieri*, one presumes; sons of men of letters bought newspapers or became professors, and so on. That society still exists, and very powerful it is. But it is not what it was. Partly overtaken by economic growth, partly by its own conscience, partly by clever young men who do not quite know the ancient rules, it is beginning, one cannot say to dissolve, but at least to become a little frayed at the edges. The present President does not come from the heart of the circle, nor did the three unknown colonels who drove the aristocratic lady back to her knitting in 1967. It is distasteful to use the events of 1967 as an argument in favour of social mobility, but they are some sort of evidence for its existence.

In Antiquity, as in most aristocratic societies, the nobleman exerted his influence, played the game of politics, made money, through that vertical, familial, mainly locally-based structure of which we have spoken. He received many little bits of support — one sword here, or one vote there — from below in exchange for general support by him from above for the area's or the clan's interests, together with a few personal favours.

Greece in 1833 was ideally suited, geographically as always, politically and socially by its more recent history, for the operation of this primitive system. The Turks themselves, not to mention the Franks before them, had even encouraged the development under their general suzerainty. That suzerainty removed, there was little the new Greek governments could do to impose their authority, though they tried hard enough, except to build up a new structure which, at village or township level, could not be much more than cosmetic. To take the extreme example, when the first properly elected Greek parliament was instituted under the Constitution of 1862, it was on paper a splendid example of democratic constitutional propriety. And it was indeed a splendid thing. But, under the umbrella of international democratic applause, it was much easier for the local boss (though now operating on a wider scale) to smuggle into it the established habits of thought from his village than it was for central government to change the manners of the village. The idea of patronage was simply absorbed into the Parliamentary system and has remained there. Local ties, local loyalties were what mattered, and they still do.

Not very many years ago, the people of a certain village in the Peloponnese found themselves without a candidate for Parliament. They had always been represented by a member of the same family, and so they turned to that family again. But there came a shock. The only available member of the family was a Communist while his predecessors and their supporters had always been men of the right. Incredibly to us, though it should not be so incredible after what I have been saying, the shock affected the liberated young man of national affiliations far more than it affected his would-be constituents. They simply invited him to stand. Astonished and reluctant he stood, was elected, and thereafter exerted his patronage, or shall we say, did his duty by his constituents no less loyally than his forbears. The same spirit grew to inhabit the higher levels of politics. In a survey among Greek members of parliament carried out not long before the coup of 1967 on the subject of what they regarded as necessary qualities for ministerial office, between twenty and twenty-five per cent of those questioned cited 'political strength, intelligence and moral qualities'. But roughly the same number still mentioned 'patronage'. Only 'specialist knowledge' rated higher, at thirty-five per cent, and this was at a time when the younger Papandreou had already done much to sell to the Greeks his new idea of the Kennedy-type whiz kid. It was all summed up a long time ago by Kolletis, Prime Minister in the 1840s and past-master of the patronage game, who promised posts in the government to all and gave them to none. 'In making any appointment', he said, 'I make one friend and twenty enemies.'

Patronage and nepotism are not necessarily dirty words. In a society which has no other means already fashioned to control the political game, they are simply a fact of life, neither good nor bad, and no one should criticise the Greeks for behaving as they had to behave and to some extent still have to behave. The words acquire dirtiness only as new, not by definition better, methods come to be accepted, to be taken gradually as the norm. The methods of the western European party system are, I think, though by no means perfect, better, just as the individually based interest methods of the fifth century B.C. were better than the patronage methods of the sixth century or before. Therefore, I (but I stress *I*) prefer them, and so, on this point too, feel happy to see changes in the practices of modern Greek politics, to see signs of – here again we meet that imperfect word – class-thinking creeping in. Old manners are being eroded, even if only by improved communications; the appeal of Andreas Papandreou, and his own reputed expertise are one clear sign, but there are two more striking still.

After the awful horrors of the German occupation, and the still more awful agony of the Civil War, it is not surprising that the fragile framework of the Greek central government could not take the strain. There was chaos, and it was not surprising that at the General Elections of 1950 no fewer than forty-four parties presented themselves at the polls, including one that called itself the Motorists of Greece. There's imagination for you. That party won one hundred and fifty-seven votes and no seats. But nine other parties did less well. Democracy? Thanks in the first place to the astuteness of the leaders of the main Right Wing party, General Papagos and his advisers, and later to his successor Mr Karamanlis, whose lead was soon followed by George Papandreou in the centre and by Partsalides on the left, these forty-four parties had reduced themselves to three, in effect, by 1964, and there would have been three again in 1967 had the *coup* not happened. That is something more like it. Forty-four to three — an amazing change.

Even more interesting is the aftermath of the *coup* of 1967. That *coup* I felt and frequently forecast, would send Greece back, when the dictatorship fell, as it had to fall, to the chaos of 1951. Some confusion there has been and will continue to be, especially on the left, but it is trivial in comparison with what could be feared and trivial by comparison with the smoothness, ease and good sense with which in general constitutional government has been reestablished. That is the measure of how Greek attitudes have changed, and have changed too, on the last of the three points, reverence for the πολιτεία, the νόμοι, for the Constitution. The first formal Constitution of 1844 was a farce, owing more to international fashion than anything real in Greece. The French and American Revolutions were still recent news and have much responsibility to bear for it. The first real Constitution of 1862 still had its air of unreality, though it lasted with several hiccups, serious hiccups, for quite a long time. The Constitution of 1952 was still not perfect, but the significant point is that, when the revolutionaries of 1967 were expelled and their pseudo-constitution of 1968 was dismissed, it meant a return to 1952, not another return to the drawing-board. 'Bad laws which are stable are better than good laws which are always being changed.' We remember the words of Cleon in 427 B.C. Soon, when imperfections are removed, they will be removed constitutionally, not by force.

That then, is the argument. Behind it all lies the principle that if a day or even an hour is a long time in politics, twenty or even a hundred years is a short time in political history. Classical Greece did not appear in an hour, or even a week. It took more than two hundred years. Nor were they years of steady progress. There were moments of what must have seemed like disaster. How did Solon feel when he saw his own attempts at a Constitution suspended by his old political ally Peisistratus, thirty years or so after its creation? Solon himself had previously said that tyranny was a nice enough position, but that there was no way out of it. That was a bit too gloomy, but tyranny in Athens did last on and off for nearly fifty years. A century later, Athens shrugged off two artificial attempts at tyranny in a matter of months.

It is against this background of extended time that we look for progress. Not regular, but rather two steps forward one step back in the three directions I have proposed. And those periods of progress, not of ultimate achievement, we call archaic. To me, unlike the editor of the Oxford English dictionary, 'archaic' is a friendly word, a word of hope. I should like to have lived in Greece in the sixth century B.C. I should not be unhappy living in Greece today.

3 Homer Today

Malcolm Willcock

Homer is both the oldest of the Greek poets and the one whose impact is eternally new. Why should this be so? Why did the *Iliad* dominate the ancient world in literature and thought? Why is it so significant to modern literature? Why do people accept as an orthodoxy that Homer and Shakespeare are 'the greatest of the poets'? Why do so many school-children in our country, and university students, long to learn ancient Greek, impelled by a specific urge to reach a certain goal, to be able to read Homer in the original?

Is it possible to define and specify the qualities of the *Iliad*? Why has it this continuing attraction and influence?

It is an interesting fact that in this sort of discussion 'Homer' indicates the *Iliad*, and the *Odyssey* is disregarded. This is true in the present case, although it might well be thought that the *Odyssey* would be more appropriate to a series of lectures on 'Greece Old and New', for the *Odyssey* is pre-eminently about the Greek world, with its islands and harbours, and the intelligent Greek people, aware of themselves and interested in the doings of strangers. The *Iliad* is different; it is more universal. One has to say of it that it is not particularly about Greece or the Greek people, but about all humanity, all people and all time. This is a point to which we shall return.

In consideration and discussion of the *Iliad*, we in the English-speaking world have been confused and bemused in recent years. We have lost sight of the great qualities, and concentrated on small details, on what are called the 'formulas', two- or three-word phrases, which are the building blocks making up the lines of the verse. In the discussion of these we have been in danger of failing to see the wood for the trees, of losing our perception of the quality of the poet.

This tendency has recently started to change.[1] In line with that, I propose to aim here for two goals, one technical and one general. The technical goal is to consider an important distinction in the interpretation of Homer, between explanations based on what are called 'recurrent themes', and explanations that assume intentional composition. The more general aim is to put into words something of the quality of Homer, with an argument for unique and individual genius.

The *Iliad* is a huge epic of twenty-four books, containing about 16,000 lines. It would take three days to recite, we are told. Its dramatic subject is the anger of Achilleus, and the harm his quarrel with Agamemnon did to the Greek army at Troy; but in addition to this dramatic, even psychological, plot, it contains a great deal of narrative, mostly about fighting, and of heroic and human behaviour. To interpret this long poem, and explain its genesis, there have been four main lines of approach.

Two of the approaches are traditional, opposed to each other, the two poles of scholarship, going back to (and even beyond)[2] the *Prolegomena ad Homerum* of Friedrich Wolf (1795), and so for some 200 years. They are the approach of the 'analysts' and that of the 'unitarians'. Homeric scholars have in the past been divided into these two categories, and they still are, although the last fifty years have produced two effective new approaches, as we shall see.

The analysts were fine scholars who knew the *Iliad* well, and by the power of intelligence and discrimination felt able to judge, according to various criteria, between early and late, old and new, within the epic; that is to say, they found distinct *stages* of composition. Essential therefore to their position was that there was no single author, and consequently their arguments had the aim of destroying the apparent unity of the work. They were ruthless men. Not for them the vision of one composer, which others may feel they see, nor the overall coherence of a character and his actions; they delighted in discovering inconsistency and incoherence. These scholars have been mostly German or (in recent times) Swiss. They carry weight by their distinction. They have not had great influence in Britain, however, owing partly to our less logical habits of mind, our national tendency towards empiricism, and partly to what might to an outsider seem perilously close to laziness.

The only analyst who wrote in English, who is significant for us today, is Walter Leaf, and that because he was the author of the main library edition of the *Iliad*, and co-author of the school edition based on it, that of Leaf and Bayfield.[3] This edition has recently gone out of print, and so will gradually cease to be used. It has been strange in recent decades to realise that many students were learning to read Homer with the help of a commentary which preceded all modern understanding of the poet, and instructed them that whole books of the *Iliad*, or parts of books, are late and poor additions; it began the notes on Book 8, for example, with the words, 'Of all the books in the *Iliad* there can be no doubt that Theta [Book 8] is the least original'. And so on. They say that Book 8 has been added to the poem to provide an introduction for Book 9 (the Embassy); and Book 9 itself is (again according to Leaf and Bayfield), 'one of the very latest additions to the *Iliad*'.

Opposed to the analysts were, and are, the scholars who are called unitarians. Essentially of course they believe in a single poet. They see his artistry and his understanding. And insist on these against, or in spite of, or in ignorance of, all the evidence to the contrary set out by the analysts. For example, the unitarians will naturally draw attention to those parts of the *Iliad* which contain the most feeling and understanding of humanity: Books 1, 6, 9, 18, 24 (the quarrel between Achilleus and Agamemnon in 1; the farewell between Hektor and Andromache in 6; the speeches of Achilleus and Phoinix in 9; the scene between Achilleus and his mother in 18, after the death of Patroklos; and the scene between Achilleus and Priam in 24, when the old king of Troy has come to the Greek camp to ransom the body of his son). A unitarian scholar will try to point out the common quality of these scenes, and thus the identity of the mind which created them; and to argue that there is one poet. The analysts on the contrary, as we saw just now, tend to treat the Embassy in 9 as late, and almost to a man they argue that 24 is a very late addition to the poem indeed, a view for which they produce detailed linguistic arguments.

So these two schools, or not so much schools as attitudes, are in total contrast to each other. And it used to be said that on the whole the best scholars were analysts; the poets and lovers of literature were unitarians.

The last fifty years have seen two important new approaches which have radically changed the picture.

The first is so well known now that it has become the orthodoxy in English-speaking lands, and thus healthily subject to criticism and refinement; namely, the view of the Homeric epics as examples of *oral poetry*. This stems from the comparative study of heroic literatures, and brings into the discussion the qualitative difference between the method of production of oral poetry and that of poetry which is composed with the aid of writing. It began, or at least the impact on *our* Homeric studies began, with the American scholar Milman Parry, exactly fifty years ago. That was the year (1928) of Parry's Paris dissertations, *L'Épithète Traditionnelle dans Homère* and *Les Formules et la Métrique d'Homère*.[4] His lesson was that the obvious repetitions in the Homeric style are caused by 'formulaic composition', that is the composition in phrases or groups of words filling a given part of the hexameter line, instead of in individual words. This, if true and pervasive through the epics, as it seems to be, is evidently a major difference from the method of such as Vergil and Milton; and immediately gives a totally new picture of the *nature* of Homeric verse. The formulas are the units in the repertoire of the poet from which he creates his lines; and they are subject to a fairly stringent principle of economy, whereby he does not unnecessarily vary the formulas, but repeats the same phrases as and when they are required.

Milman Parry's successor, Professor A. B. Lord, took the oral poetry theory one stage further, by pointing out that repetition occurs in the subject matter of the poems as well as in the diction, and that here again oral composition provides the explanation. The poet had a stock of story patterns, descriptions, incidents, and so on, which were as available to him for the composition of his tale as the formulas were for the composition of his verses. This is all of course set out in Lord's excellent book *The Singer of Tales*.[5] To these elements for the composition of the stories the rather imprecise term 'themes' has been given. Examples of a theme are: the arming of a hero, which comes four times in the *Iliad*, with recognisably the same sequence of description; the soliloquy of a hero in a position of danger, again found four times in the poem; Nestor's typical tales of his youthful prowess; Polydamas' speeches of advice to his coeval Hektor. Each of these also comes, strangely enough, exactly four times in our *Iliad*. And study has shown that in every case the poet is working to a pattern, modifying the description or the speech according to the peculiar circumstances of the present, but (in the words of Lewis Carroll), 'still keeping one principal object in view, to preserve its symmetrical shape'. The conclusion is drawn that these patterns existed in the poet's mind, available for use when required: the story reaches a certain point, and the circumstances 'trigger off' a response from the poet, which takes the form of a stock description, or theme.

Thus the picture is of a professional bard, with a well-stocked repertoire built up during his apprenticeship or later, not of actual poems, but of formulas and themes, from which he could, on request, produce the public performance of a mythological tale. Two general principles about poetry of this sort were laid down in the course of the discussion, namely that (1) the poet must be illiterate; and (2) there can be no fixed text. The song is created anew each time the poet sings it. He may indeed stay very close to the way he sang it last time, but he has not memorised it, and there is no concept of verbatim accuracy.

How we can equate these principles, of the illiterate poet and the impossibility of a fixed text, with the existence and survival of the *Iliad*, is the major problem still facing Homeric scholars.

Let us return, however, to the general discussion of oral poetry and its nature. The new approach is obviously of the utmost importance. It has changed our whole understanding of Homer. It took some time to affect us in Britain, in spite of the common language; on the continent it took longer, infiltrating first through Holland, and then with an outpost in Austria, before it invaded the analytical stronghold of Germany itself.

We simply cannot understand some features of the artificial language of Homer without appreciating the effect of a tradition of oral poetry. And of course it totally explains the repetition of phrases, line and groups of lines in the *Iliad*. Part of the old analytical method was to discuss which of two occurrences of a line or set of lines was the original and which the later copy. We can now see that that is virtually meaningless in a world of formulas and themes. The beginning of Leaf and Bayfield's commentary on Book 8 of the *Iliad*, the opening sentence of which was quoted above, goes on (after 'Of all the books of the *Iliad*, there can be no doubt that Theta is the least original'), 'Large parts at a time are made up of lines, and even whole speeches, taken bodily from other parts of the *Iliad*.' We can now see that the assumption here is fallacious. They are not taken, or at least we have no reason to suppose that they were taken, from other parts of the *Iliad*. The repetition derives from the normal compositional method of the poet.

This is all very important, but it does not explain Homer. This is the impasse we have reached in recent years. The more one, considers formulas and themes, the more one begins to see Homer as little more than a good technician, who was adept in the use of pre-existing materials, who was well trained and had learned his art. A computer could do as well, if properly programmed. But Pope said, 'Homer had the greatest Invention of any poet whatsoever',[6] and this was the natural view of the ancient world, its other poets, its literary critics, its commentators. There is a clear incompatibility between the repetitive formulaic poet now discovered and the inventive genius admired in the past.

This brings us to the fourth school, the second of the two important new approaches of the last fifty years. It is a continental approach, relatively little known in this country. The scholars in question mostly call themselves neo-analysts. To put it simply, they analyse the text of the *Iliad* with the same attention as their predecessors, the old-style analysts, but come up with the diametrically opposite answer. They find the hand of the individual poet; they see Homer at work.

There is a slight difficulty about the definition of what in fact the neo-analysts do. It is simplest to distinguish two separate lines of approach. The first is to deduce from internal evidence in the *Iliad* what connections Homer may have had with poetry that preceded him; what were his models? and did he change things when he created his own story? This is a very subtle approach, and obviously dangerous, as the only evidence we have for what pre-Homeric poetry was like has to be deduced from the *Iliad* itself. A leader in this field is the present-day Greek scholar John Kakridis, Emeritus Professor from Thessalonica. Perhaps his most important book is written in English, namely *Homeric Researches*, published at Lund in Sweden in 1949. (This book is now regrettably out of print.) The great value of this approach is that in explaining surprising or disconcerting or illogical features of the tale as it is told in Homer, it brings in as a hypothesis other material that may have conditioned Homer's version, and particularly parallel mythological situations. We can of course deduce with certainty that heroic verse was sung before the *Iliad*. If we see in the *Iliad* a scene which is hardly convincing in its present context, but would be eminently so in another, we may well think that the other context, which has not survived, is logically prior to the one which has. There is no reason why both should not have been part of the same poet's repertoire. So we are not necessarily talking of Homer imitating some predecessor's work; it may have been a matter of conflation of material within his own mind. The most obvious example of this is that many scenes in the latter part of the *Iliad* which deal with the death and funeral of Patroklos have a close resemblance to what we know from other sources was said to have happened at the death and funeral of Achilleus himself. The neo-analytical argument is that what was more significant came first, and we have in the *Iliad* a reflection, in the minor key, of images and scenes which pre-existed as part of the major story. Some may consider that this does not prove very much. But in practice it brings us closer to understanding the habit of mind and the method of Homer; and that is something indeed.

The second line of approach of the neo-analysts is pure unitarianism, the argument for single authorship based on structural and other connections within the work. Here we owe an immense debt to Wolfgang Schadewaldt's Iliasstudien[7] and to a lesser extent to Karl Reinhardt's *Die Ilias und ihr Dichter*.[8] Schadewaldt had the intense insight of a great scholar, and could show that a proper study of the detail of the *Iliad* led, not to a sense of confusion and inconsistency, but to one of consistency and creative power. In fact, he was the direct opposite of the older analysts. His main achievement is in pointing out the parallels, the cross-references, the foreshadowing of one scene by another, the preparation of his story by the poet as he goes along, so that little touches are brought in in advance which bear fruit later. He demonstrates the artistry of the design, and from it the evidence for the single mind.

As an example, it was Schadewaldt who rescued Book 8 from the vulnerable position it had reached in the hands of the analysts, as in the sentences quoted above from the notes of Leaf and Bayfield. It will be remembered that they treated Book 8 as a book inserted merely to prepare the way for Book 9, itself a late addition to the *Iliad*. Schadewaldt shows clearly that on the contrary Book 8 is an essential part of the composition of the *Iliad*. It is in fact the turning point of the battle, for it is in Book 8 that Zeus first starts to fulfil the promise made in Book 1, that he would help the Trojans to defeat the Greeks, and so compel them to apologise to Achilleus. Schadewaldt's method is to consider various aspects of the book, and check their points of contact with other parts of the *Iliad*; and if he finds, as he does, that Book 8 is connected with, and indeed is essential to, much of the rest, the cumulative evidence is over-whelming that it is an original and organic part of the whole.

In Book 8 Hektor loses two charioteers. The position of a charioteer was itself a vulnerable one, because, as the chariots are used for transport in the *Iliad*, not for fighting, it is the function of the charioteer to drive his passenger to the front, where he dismounts to fight, and then to keep the chariot as close as possible in case of a sudden wish to leave that scene on the part of the hero he serves. So they would usually either be carrying their fighter to the action or manoeuvring the chariot and horses just behind the front line. It is thus clear that it was particularly dangerous to be charioteer to a fighter who took risks; and Hektor was pre-eminently a fighter who took risks.

So in Book 8 Hektor's charioteer Eniopeus is killed at line 123. Hektor grieved for him, but immediately found a replacement, Archeptolemos. The sequence is repeated at line 315. Archepto-lemos is killed, and in the same set of lines (composition by theme and by formula) Hektor grieved for him, but immediately found a replacement. And the replacement this time is Hektor's own brother Kebriones. Now this repetition has two effects. One is to show the dangers Hektor ran. In both cases the weapon which killed the charioteer was actually aimed at Hektor. His rash fighting is shown by the fact that nobody else in the *Iliad* loses two charioteers. It also pinpoints Kebriones. What chance are we to suppose that he has of surviving to Book 24? And in fact Kebriones is going to play a major role for a short time at the turning point of the whole *Iliad*, in Book 16. That is where the epic has changed from battle story to personal tragedy, when Achilleus has sent out his friend Patroklos to help the hard-pressed Greeks. Kebriones is the last named person to be killed in Book 16 by Patroklos before the death of Patroklos himself; and the battle rages over his body, and Homer uses for him the most memorable epitaph for a dead warrior in the whole epic – in Lattimore's translation, 'He in the turning dust lay / mightily in his might, his horsemanship all for-gotten'.[9] Kebriones is a key figure then; and already in Book 8 he was being simply and directly brought to our attention. The poet was aware in Book 8 of what he was going to do in Book 16. And why not? But this totally contradicts the view of the analysts that Book 8 is a late addition to the story. It may be noticed also that Kebriones, who after all is not an important person, not a great hero, has no other function except to be the temporary charioteer of Hektor, is mentioned in passing in every book of fighting between Books 8 and 16. Homer did not want us to lose sight of him. This is what is called foreshadowing, the preparation of the minds of the audience for what is to come, so that when it comes there is recognition, not surprise. The device of a skilled story-teller.

That is an example of the neo-analytical approach, analysing detail and finding the mind of the poet. Of course it is not new. It is a reversion to the ways of the ancient critics, as seen in the scholia; they were not in the least doubt of the inventive creativity of the poet. It is also a reaction against the over-cleverness, and indeed when one comes down to it, the simple-mindedness, of the old-style analysts.

There are many other examples where one can see the mind of the poet and story-teller, preparing the sequence of events, appreciating the human reactions of the characters, making everything probable and consequential, as Aristotle later recommended.[10] If we consider the wounding of the minor heroes Machaon and Eurypylos in Book 11, planned to provide a reason for first sending Patroklos from Achilleus to Nestor, and then delaying his return, or the way Antilochos's situation at the edge of the battle is mentioned early in Book 17 to get him into our minds for the message that he must take later in the same book, we will see that we have a story-teller firmly in control, and intelligently anticipating the later stages of his narrative. And again why not? But this is something different from the consecutive layers of composition discovered by the analysts.

These two attitudes − oral poetry theory and neo-analysis − come from the new world of America and the old world of Europe. We are located somewhere in the middle, and have the possible advantage of taking account of both. For they do not have much direct contact; and often they will look at the same passage and offer different explanations. There may be a scene, fitting tightly into the plot, which can be interpreted either as a typical 'recurrent theme' triggered off in the poet's mind by the external situation, or as a significant part of the creative poet's structural design, depending on whether the interpreter comes from America or from central Europe. For example, take this pair of events:

A. At the beginning of Book 1, the old priest Chryses comes to the Greek camp in an attempt to ransom his daughter; he is roughly turned away by Agamemnon. There ensue the quarrel between Achilleus and Agamemnon and the consequent disasters of the *Iliad*.

B. At the beginning of Book 24, the old king Priam comes to the Greek camp in an attempt to ransom the body of his son; he is politely received by Achilleus. There ensue the relaxation of the anger of Achilleus and the peaceful end to the *Iliad*.

How do we interpret the similarity between these two situations, placed almost as boundary markers at the beginning and end of the poem? Oral poetry theory might argue that we have a stock situation, part of the poet's repertoire, repeated when he felt the urge from poem to poem. The old weak father and the powerful young man of violence, who has no reason except his own whim to do anything that he is asked: this is a natural pattern for story-telling. There is a similar situation in Scott's *Ivanhoe*, where old Isaac of York comes to offer money to rescue his daughter Rebecca from the dreadful Templar. This attitude, that it is a natural theme for a story, sees no particular connection between Chryses in Book 1 and Priam in Book 24. They are merely two examples of a common situation, allomorphs of a single *Gestalt*, as the dreadful jargon has it. The other attitude to Chryses and Priam trying at either end of the poem to ransom their live daughter and dead son respectively, is to see in it evidence of the creative poet's art. The end of the tale reflects and corrects the beginning. Achilleus, when his anger is evaporating and peaceful feelings are taking its place, shows pity for the old man, whereas Agamemnon was without pity or consideration, in the fierceness of his pride and power. And in this repetition and amendment the *Iliad* may well be said to teach a moral lesson. And that is a strong argument for unity of authorship.[11]

This is the distinction towards which much of the previous discussion was tending, the distinction between the alternative kinds of explanation offered by the oral poetry theorists and the neo-analysts. There is an opportunity perhaps to see that the two alternatives are not mutually exclusive; that both may simultaneously be true; that if we can at the same time observe repeated themes and also the creative invention of the poet, we are getting nearer to Homer, and using our geographical position more or less midway between Harvard and Thessalonica to good effect.

These modern approaches, then, taken together, help our understanding of the poet. He uses the techniques and devices of oral composition, and therefore we can deduce that he was himself of that tradition, an oral bard. But we have also argued that he is a conscious literary artist. There is a balancing between the beginning and the end of the long work; and there is a pervasive technique of preparation, of foreshadowing, which shows the story-teller in full control of his tale.

Is there anything else we can tell about the mind of Homer? What about his relationship to the tradition of heroic verse which we can be quite sure preceded him? Is he to be treated as an example of that tradition, or is he different?

The supreme quality of the *Iliad* lies, in my opinion, in the observation of character and behaviour. Others might propose other qualities. The construction of the whole, with the plot of the Anger of Achilleus and its devastating effects, the anger aroused in Book 1, hardened in the Embassy scene in Book 9, transferred to Hektor in Book 18, fulfilled by Hektor's death in Book 22, and evaporating in the humane scene with Priam in Book 24, this is surely the construction of a very superior mind. Or again there is the detail — most exact descriptions produced by a vivid visual imagination, so that it is clear that the poet is most precisely envisaging what he is describing. This quality is the reason why some have felt great doubts about the ancient story that Homer was blind; at least, they feel, he cannot always have been blind.

But I would put the characters, the relationships, the observation of human behaviour, above either of these other qualities. There are, for a start, those strongly drawn, individually recognisable heroes, mostly Greek, but including also some Trojans and allies. They are just as basic to the plot as the anger of Achilleus. The Greek leaders are introduced to us in all their individuality in the early books, especially Books 3 and 4, and from then on our recognition of their personalities is reinforced by their behaviour throughout the story, until we see them for the last time in the funeral games of Book 23, still acting in accordance with the individual character of each. It is evident that in the action, in the books of fighting and in those funeral games, Homer has chosen incidents primarily to demonstrate character, not merely for the excitement of the events themselves. This is true of the major characters obviously, such as Odysseus, Diomedes, Nestor, Agamemnon, Menelaos, the two Aiantes, and so on; but also of the relatively minor characters, such as Meriones or Antilochos. Whether we consciously notice it or not, a pattern of behaviour is established for each one, and a great part of the persuasiveness of the narrative derives from the appropriateness of the actions to the characters who perform them.

How much of this is to be ascribed to Homer personally, and how much to the tradition? It is certain, for example, that Odysseus and Agamemnon were the subjects of poetry before Homer, and Nestor and others as well. Do we think that their characters have been modified by Homer, that there is a new subtlety in his presentation of them? Or is it something that was built up in the world of formulas and themes? Essentially, what was Achilleus like before the *Iliad*? Was he moody and introspective? What was Agamemnon like? Was he blustering and small-minded? Or were they simpler figures, great heroes of vivid and violent achievements, admirable, superior and remote?

These may seem difficult questions, to be answered only on the basis of subjective judgement and prejudice. But in fact we do have some evidence about the nature of the characters in the tradition before Homer. It lies in the stock epithets which are attached to the heroes' names, and preserved in the fossilized phraseology of the formulas. It is clear, when one thinks about it, that the stock epithets do not describe the heroes in their rounded Homeric existence, but present qualities and attributes which distinguish them from their fellows on a much more superficial level. For example, the stock epithets tell us that Agamemnon was 'king of men' and 'lord of wealthy Mykenai', and that Achilleus was 'swift-footed' and 'sacker of cities'. The irresoluteness, however, of the one, and the moodiness of the other, are not to be found in the stock epithets.

It seems very probable that here we have a difference between Homer and the tradition; he has turned the heroic figures of legend into human beings. Hektor is another good example. The man we admire is not the fighting and killing Hektor of the middle books ('man-slaying Hektor'), but the Hektor who is said briefly at the end to have been kind to Helen, the Hektor who takes to his heels and runs when Achilleus comes near in Book 22. That is an amazing fact. In an epic about fighting heroes, and personal honour and bravery, we feel no criticism of Hektor when his nerve breaks and he runs away. Why not? Because we know about Andromache, and we have just heard the appeals of Priam and Hekabe.

And the example of Hektor shows that our concern is not always with the characters as independent figures; there is also the question of relationships. And here we move to a still higher level, a level of universality, where Homer shows a broad awareness of the human condition. They may be kings and queens and mighty heroes, but what we see and react to are the most simple and basic relationships: a young husband with his wife and baby; an old father and mother very proud of their grown-up son, and intensely concerned for him; the protectiveness of an elder brother; the unthinking loyalty of friends to each other in the fighting. These are the things that justify the earlier comment that the *Iliad* is of all people and all time, not just of the Greeks, and certainly not just of the heroic age.

It looks as if we have identified a real difference. Whether it is totally innovation by Homer, or whether there had been a softening and civilising among the Ionian poets in the school to which he belonged, we cannot tell. But in Homer compared with the past tradition of heroic verse, we may deduce a qualitative difference. The traditional heroes have been humanised, turned into men recognisably like, but better than, ourselves, as Aristotle recommended for the heroes of tragedy.[12] And this change, from heroic to human, is an essential aspect of Homer's interest in human character and behaviour, and of his portrayal of the most basic and simple human relationships.

NOTES

1. A more literary approach is to be found in J. Griffin, 'Homeric Pathos and Objectivity' and 'The Divine Audience and the Religion of the Iliad', in *The Classical Quarterly*, xxvi (1976) pp. 161−87 and xxviii (1978) pp. 1−22; and particularly in the growing frequency of reference in scholarly literature to Simone Weil's 'The Iliad, or The Poem of Force' (published in France in 1940; English translation by Mary McCarthy in the November 1945 issue of *Politics*).
2. For the point made here, as well as the general history of the Homeric Question, *see* G. Broccia, *La Questione Omerica* (Florence, 1979).
3. W. Leaf, *The Iliad* (London, 1st edn 1886−8; 2nd edn 1900−2); W. Leaf and M. A. Bayfield, *The Iliad of Homer* (London, 1895−8).
4. The writings of Milman Parry have been reprinted (and where applicable translated into English) by his son Adam Parry in *The Making of Homeric Verse* (Oxford, 1971).
5. A. B. Lord, *The Singer of Tales* (Cambridge, Mass., 1960).
6. Alexander Pope, in the first sentence of the Preface to his translation of the *Iliad* (London, 1715).

7. Wolfgang Schadewaldt, *Iliasstudien* 1st edn (Leipzig, 1938).
8. Karl Reinhardt, *Die Ilias und ihr Dichter* (Göttingen, 1961).
9. *Iliad*, 16.775–6. R. Lattimore's translation is published by the Chicago University Press (1951).
10. Aristotle, *Poetics*, ch. 9.
11. In *Our Mutual Friend* the mature Charles Dickens does something very like this. Lizzie Hexam, who is shown in the opening scenes as oarswoman to her father in his disreputable activities on the Thames, uses her skill with the oars to save her lover Eugene Wrayburn at the end of the book; and the gentle Mr Twemlow, whose unsureness on all subjects is portrayed at the beginning, comes out with the decisive moral judgement in the final scene.
12. Aristotle, *Poetics*, chs 13, 15.

4 Migration and Assimilation in Greece

Nicholas Hammond

The migration of the Albanians is the best attested and in many ways the most instructive of migrations into Greece. I first met Albanians in 1930 on a cold January day on the coast of Epidaurus coming down from hills to a hill village when the light was just beginning to fail. In the village square there were two men dressed in bear skins doing a bear dance around each other, and all the villagers were in the square watching it. When we came through the houses into the square everyone ran away and when we asked about it they denied that there had been any dancing. This is an old January custom which had persisted in this village. We had difficulty staying because they were rather suspicious of us, but we stayed with a man who talked Greek as his main language, although he talked to his wife in Albanian. His son had just come back from Athens having been conscripted into the army, and the son said how stupid these old folk were and how little they knew about life. He had come back from Athens full of ideas, and he said that in Athens there was no need for conversation, as it was all done by gesture. So he gestured to me, and I gestured to him, and we did the most elaborate gestures, and the old man watched us with his eyes popping and then said to us, 'What were you saying to each other?' and then of course his son produced a thoroughly elaborate conversation. This is an interesting example of migration and assimilation. The ancestors of these people probably came to Epidaurus in the fourteenth or fifteenth century, but they were still talking Albanian as their mother tongue in 1930. They were bilingual with the males talking Greek mainly and the females talking Albanian mainly, and the sons, having become conscripts and lived in Athens, passing altogether out of the Albanian sphere. In 1979 there would probably be no one in that village, apart from the very old, who would know a word of Albanian.

That same year I went to the area which is called Tsamouria, which is in Epirus near the Albanian border (the area which the Italians made a pretext for invading Greece in 1940), and there I stayed with a family which was a normal Albanian family unit of about thirty or forty people, all with sons and wives living together in this large family group. They were agriculturalists. Albanian was the language they talked among themselves, but they could also talk Greek. This was their second language, although they lived in Greece.

Both these groups regarded themselves as entirely Greek. The one in Epirus which was still Albanian in its customs and its language had probably been there since about 1400. I went into Albania the same year and I stayed with Albanians in villages in the Kurvelesh, the most backward part of southern Albania inland behind the mountains. The houses I stayed in were built like fortresses, with slit windows, because they had so many vendettas. The vendettas are within the circles of kindred. The circles express family kinships, groups of families forming a *phratry* (brotherhood) and living in what is called a *mahala* (part of a big village). The village itself is a group of related families living in its scattered parts. They would themselves be part of a tribe, and there are vendettas between families, between persons, and between tribes.[1]

In Albania you have the source of many of those things which I saw in the Tsamouria and in Epidaurus, or for that matter in many of the villages of Attica. The basis of life in Albania is the family and the tribe, the tribes being very numerous and very small. The system was exactly the same in Antiquity in Epirus, even in Hellenistic times. Tribalism still exists in Albania, or did in the 1930s, and you can see the offshoots of it. The problem I hope to deal with is how did the Albanians get from this remote part of the Kurvelesh down to all parts of the Greek peninsula, and indeed the islands, and how far and how were they assimilated?

Let me begin by looking at the country over which we are going to bring these people from Albania to Greece.[2] This area of country that I am going to talk mainly about lies between the

Aegean Sea and the Adriatic by Durazzo and as far south as Corfu. The Macedonian area is governed by the great rivers, the Vardar and the Haliacmon. The area of greatest importance from my point of view is the area of north Pindus which is a very wide area of high mountains in which the passes are all over 5000 feet high, and it is still covered by natural forest and natural alpine pastures. The best pastures are on volcanic formations called serpentine and are extremely rich. They are probably the best pastures in the Balkans, but they stop further south, when you get onto limestone and have inferior pastures. This central great area of mountain is the main pastoral area we are going to have to deal with.

The coastal plains are small in Macedonia in relation to the vast hinterland, whereas on the west side, in Albania, there is a continuous coastal plain which provides abundant winter pastures. Again in Epirus there are a certain number of coastal plains which provide the winter pasture. Now the particular form of pastoralism that we shall be dealing with is what is called transhumant pastoralism, in which great numbers of sheep and a certain number of goats are kept; they spend six months in the summer on the alpine pastures, and they then move down to the coast and spend six months on the coastal pastures. These sheep are kept for milking; you sit behind a sheep and milk it between its legs, as you may have seen on some pieces in the exhibition of 'Scythian Gold' and the milk is the main product of the sheep. A lot of young rams are eaten at Easter, when they are very small; otherwise, the sheep are rarely eaten. They are kept also for their wool. This provides a great deal of the shepherd's clothing, and the women make and sell rugs. This area is the area best known for this form of transhumant pastoralism, which involves movements to the mountains in summer and in the winter down to the plains.

Behind the coast at Durazzo are the main Albanian mountains, covered in snow until late spring. By Lake Ohrid and Lake Prespa is the high mountain area which is a block from the north and is very difficult for migrants to circumvent. They circumvent it along the coast by Lake Skodra near Skutari: otherwise they have to go right over to the Macedonian side in order to get through it. Further north is Montenegro which again is a great mountain mass. East of Ohrid and Prespa is an area where a great plain begins. It runs down through narrows near Bitola, the Monastir gap, as it is called, into the Lyncus province. This is the main entry into the southern part of the Balkans. The Germans came through here in 1941. There are many parallel ranges, but here again there are very good summer pastures on this high ground. Going further to the east, we come to the Vardar, passing through what is called the Demir Kapu, or the Iron Gates, which, if you go by road, is now a tunnel. This was impassable in antiquity, so that anyone who came through the Monastir gap and wanted to get to Salonica had to go down by the route through Lyncus and past Lake Ostrovo. The second German force came not via Demir Kapu, but through from the Strumica valley, crossed the hills at Valandovo, and so descended into Macedonia.

Further south on the west coast, are the great coastal plains, which are called the Malakaster, and then you get into an area of parallel mountain ranges which are closely pinched, and have routes running south, but quite difficult routes at times. Then in the centre of the peninsula you have a high mountain area which is the main pasture area. This area too is full of defiles and gorges, such as the Aoi Stena, and again you are into the mountains very quickly. Leading south from the plateau near the Lake of Ioannina a series of valleys parallel to the coast all lead you southwards. Inland again you have the high mountains which afford the summer pastures. Then you descend to the plain of Thessaly connected by narrow valleys to the plain of Macedonia. If you are starting from the Albanian plains, you come south down these narrow valleys that get narrower and narrower. Although on your flank you have some rather well-populated areas like the big basin of Ioannina and the basin of Argyrocastro, it is probable that invaders such as the Albanians will tend to keep down near the coast.

Who were these Albanians? We first hear of them in the second century A.D. from Ptolemy who talks about people called Taulantii, who lived near Durazzo, and next to them he mentions Albani and Albanopolis, evidently their capital.[3] In the seventh century we get another mention of Albani in this area and we have mention of Dukagini, which is the family name of some Albanians who lived in this area in the fourteenth century. They are mentioned in Ragusa in documents somewhere about the ninth or tenth century. So we get a consistent tradition of there being 'Albani' or 'Arbani' in this area. Their home is described as a mountainous area which was dangerous and difficult. We hear of them also from the Crusaders. During the first Crusade in 1080, the Chanson de Roland anglicised or Frankified the name Albani

as 'Albanie' (in English 'Albany') and down in the south the name
Canina as 'Kent'. For in the First Crusade the Franks landed here
and captured Dyrrachium. The Chanson de Roland contains
these and other names of the period. Also we have mention of
bishops of the twelfth century who were called 'Arbanenses' or
'Albanenses'. So this is the area from which the Albanian name
derived. Interestingly enough the Illyrian name derives from the
same area because the 'Illyrii proprie dicti' who gave their name to
the classical Illyrians lived about the mouth of the Drin. So just as
the Greeks called these people 'Illyrii' from the southernmost
Illyrians of the time, so too the Albanians got their name in the
middle ages from the people of that language who lived furthest
south. The Albanians do not call themselves Albanians. They call
themselves Shqiptars, and no doubt the ancient Illyrians did not
call themselves Illyrians.

The Byzantine theme or province of Epirus Nova had in the
extreme north Albanians, but the rest of the area probably had a
mixed, mainly Greek-speaking people in the eleventh and twelfth
centuries. The first movement of the Albanians comes after the
fall of Constantinople to the Latins in 1204. The first evidence of
Albanians being on the move is found in various Byzantine historians, who indicate that Albanians began to be employed as
mercenaries. Because the Albanian system is based on the family,
they did not go as individual mercenaries but as troops and as
bands, tribal groups or family groups in the big sense of the family,
and they took with them their animals and their families. They
went south also as raiders, again moving *en masse*, and as
migrants, and in the thirteenth century already there is evidence
of them moving south, getting over the Shkumbi river and as time
goes on they begin to drive further and further south. They were
led by Vlachs, who often broke their way in first; thus the Vlachs
first entered Thessaly, and the Albanians came into Thessaly
later. So the threat of mass invasion grew. For migrating peoples
followed after the raiders and the mercenary groups. Further
impetus was imparted by the Serbs who set up a Serb principality
in the area of Zeta and pressed down into what is now northern
Albania.

What were the Byzantines to do in order to try and stem this
movement? First of all they counter-attacked and they invaded
what we now call central Albania, and we know the amount of loot
they got on one campaign, namely 1,200,000 sheep, 300,000 cattle

and 5000 horses. In Albania in the 1930s the whole population paid tax on 1,400,000 sheep. Thus in Byzantine times Albania had even more sheep than in the 1930s, and this means that the people were then practising transhumant pastoralism. But invasion did not solve the problem. For the Albanians went off to the hills, and were not killed. They lost much of their stock, but the loss only made them want to move to safer places and better land.

The other Byzantine device was to offer them land. This was done at the isthmus of Corinth in about 1338. A group of 10,000 Albanians with their families and their flocks appeared there, and asked if they could be admitted to the Peloponnese. They were accepted by Theodore, who was the principal ruler of the Peloponnese, and he took them on condition that they would be his soldiers and that they would cultivate the lands he gave them. So they were brought into the Peloponnese and used in that way. Again the Venetians invited them into Euboea and the Catalans invited them into Attica.[4] They came in and settled. That was in the late fourteenth and early fifteenth century, and the descendants of those people were still talking Albanian when I was in Greece in the 1930s.

But the main area of trouble and conflict was between the Albanians who were trying to get through to the south and the Greeks who were holding Old Epirus. What happened was that the Greeks drew back towards the hills; a lot of Greek-speaking people were probably Slavs at that point. They moved back into the hilly areas near Ioannina and further east, while the Albanians pushed on down the narrow valleys to the west with their flocks and herds and passed down to the place called Preveza, in southern Epirus. The name means in Albanian 'the crossing', and it was from Preveza that they crossed to Actium in Acarnania. Next they set up their own principality in Acarnania and Aetolia. Two chiefs, Demetrius and Ghin, set up the first Albanian principality. It was on the north shore on the Gulf of Corinth; they soon controlled Rhion, and the shortest crossing into the Peloponnese. They then crossed into the Peloponnese, some by force, others by invitation, as we have seen in the Isthmus area. By the middle of the fourteenth and early fifteenth century the majority of people in the Peloponnese were Albanian-speakers. They were described as occupying Elis with their flocks and herds, and we are told the sheep were most important, then pigs, then cattle, and of course they were good horsemen. They tried to seize power in the Peloponnese, but were defeated in the course of the fourteenth century. Meanwhile in Epirus the Greek-speaking peoples were holding out round Ioannina and on the Pindus; but they only held out by inviting the first Turks to help them in 1380. By 1430–40 the Turks had captured Ioannina themselves.

So for the pre-Turkish period it can be seen that, where you have the breakdown of a strong imperial system, the sprouting up of small principalities and the opportunity for these small principalities to expand, conditions are ripe for a movement of peoples who were accustomed to a migratory life of a particular kind in which the whole family migrated. Most of the transhumant peoples had no permanent residences because they were always on the move from A to B and so were ready to migrate, as Thucydides tells us at the beginning of his history. Such peoples easily move and they move *en masse*; when they settle down in a new area like the Peloponnese, that to them is home. They do not hark back to the place from which they came. No Albanian that I ever met in Greece thought of himself as an Albanian. He thought of himself as a Greek, because he lived in Greece and that is where he had his pastures or his fields. This seems to have happened from the very earliest times when migrants first came into Greece.

Next came invasion by the Turks. They met with terrific resistance from the Albanians, Skanderbeg being the hero of the Albanian resistance in the fifteenth century. Eventually the Turks won. They used the Albanians from then on as mercenaries and also as settlers of areas which were derelict. So the Albanian incursions into Greece continued under the Turkish system and went on right into the eighteenth century. It was coupled with a migration of Albanians by sea in the fifteenth and sixteenth centuries to Italy. They also went from the Albanian coast and from Epirus right round the tail of the Peloponnese and on to Samos and Cos and Rhodes, where considerable Albanian communities were established. Other Albanians spread, with the help of the Turks, into Hydra and Spetsae and Andros. There the Albanians proved to be excellent seamen, and in the Greek War of Independence they, above all, drove the Turks out. The most famous to us perhaps are Byron's Suliotes, who were entirely Albanian. The village called Paleokhori-Botsaris takes its name from the great hero of the resistance in the 1820s, Botsaris. His village was close to Suli in Epirus. The heroes of the naval war were the seamen of Spetsae and Hydra who were themselves Albanians.

So here we have a case of invasion with complete assimilation in terms of nationality and gradual assimilation in terms of language. In fact it is only universal education, conscription and modern mobility of the population which have destroyed the use of the Albanian language in Greece. But the genius of the Greeks throughout history was perhaps to be able to absorb peoples of different stocks and origins and languages and to integrate them into their own civilisation and communities.

I turn next to the other group of people, the Vlachs, who came in with the Albanians and provided leadership.[5] Whereas the Albanians are only partly transhumant, in the sense that only a proportion of the Albanians lived the entirely transhumant life, most of them engaging in some pasturing and also in agriculture, the Vlachs appear to have been professional transhumants, and the Vlach peoples probably originated in Dacia (an area north of the Danube, now Romania) and passed gradually down the spine of the Balkan peninsula, mainly on the west, but also in the east, while they practised their transhumant pastoralism. Having no permanent residences of any kind and living all day in the open, they made themselves little huts out of poles and thatch and then moved on again, men, women, children and animals going to and from summer and winter pastures. Of course they were warriors and hunters as well. They had to protect their animals from bears and wolves in the mountains and from humans in the plains, and they are tremendously tough people physically, and good riders. They were the most successful transhumant people in the Balkans. For instance we learn from the monastery at Lavra on Mount Athos that the monks let their pastures in Macedonia to three groups of transhumants, the Vlachs, the Bulgars and the Kumans. It was the Vlachs who were exempted from the taxes which were imposed on the others, not because the Vlachs were better people, but because they were more dangerous people. There is no doubt that the Vlachs were the most successful of these transhumant people. It was they who managed to acquire possession of the great Pindus area which has those magnificent pastures, and until the 1930s they owned the pastures by conquest, and also the timber, for they replanted the timber themselves. Now the government has stepped in. When they won those pastures is a matter for conjecture, but certainly they had possession by the thirteenth or fourteenth century. Because they were the most successful pastoral people, they took the leadership. They too were under pressure from the north, and it was they who led the Albanians in the first attacks into Thessaly.

There was a Jew called Benjamin of Tudela who, travelling in the middle of the twelfth century in Thessaly, came to Lamia near Thermopylae and said that the land to the north was called 'Vallachia', the land of the Vlachs, and that the people there were nimble as deer and dangerous. 'They come down and raid the towns and villages of the settled peoples, and no one can defeat them.' So they were a very capable and dangerous people at that time, and they gave leadership in that area. Another example is their alliance with the Bulgars, another pastoral people. Under Vlach leadership the Bulgars created an empire which extended from Varna on the Black Sea right through to central Albania — one of those evanescent principalities, but one of the biggest that was created at the time of the collapse of the Byzantine Empire.

The Vlachs were a different set of people from the Albanians. The Vlachs stayed in northern Greece; they did not move into the Peloponnese, or if they did they disappeared. These Vlachs are professional transhumants, and until probably the eighteenth century they did not have any villages. They had their encampments of flimsy huts wherever they made their main summer pastures or main winter pastures. In the summer they all came to the great pastures of the Pindus range and there they came to know each other. In the winter they were scattered over pastures up and down the coast from Preveza or the Gulf of Corinth right up into northern Albania, and also on the plain of Thessaly and in Macedonia. When they started building villages they built them on the summer pastures, up on Pindus, and their own traditions tell us that the villages were created by the 'synoikismos', or the gathering together of individual hut-encampments. Thus Samarina was made out of four, Perivoli out of five encampments.

Their great period of prosperity was in the eighteenth century when, under the Turks, they were favoured because they were productive people, and they traded their woollen goods and their animal products right up into central Europe and had their Vlach agents in Vienna and also in Germany. This came to an end in the nineteenth century, when the Turkish Empire began to collapse as the Byzantine Empire had done, and the Albanians got on the move again. This time they raided the Vlachs and destroyed most of their prosperity. What is left now is a very small element of Vlachs, because there were campaigns in this area during both

World Wars; and then their flocks were slaughtered by andartes of the Resistance movements and in the Civil War which ended only in 1950.

These Vlachs, who are full transhumants, have never been assimilated in terms of language. They remain Vlach-speaking, their language being a form of Romanian very close to Latin, and they only use Greek in as far as they have to. They maintain their own customs. For example, they work in wood but not in stone. They even had a wooden clock at Vovousa in 1930, when I remember seeing it working; but they employed Greek masons for any work with stone.

Alongside those Vlachs there are Vlachs who take to a partly settled life. For instance in this part of Macedonia which lies below the range of the fine pastures and descends to Grevena, you have people called 'Men of the Oak Trees', because it is a place with oak scrub. They are Vlachs who have given up the full migrant life of the transhumant and have settled down. They still raise sheep and they still pasture sheep, but they do other things also, so they are scorned by the transhumants who do not let any of them marry transhumant women. In consequence the 'Men of the Oak Trees' began to marry Greek women and their children acquired Greek speech. They are already on the way to becoming fully settled and fully integrated into the Greek speaking community. Other groups in Turkish times settled down in Thessaly. 'Farsherot Vlachs' for instance, came from a place in Albania called Farshër. By now they have become traders. They were absorbed into normal nineteenth-century life and now into twentieth-century life.

We have looked at three stages or kinds of assimilation. In the first there was very little assimilation, but the incomers quickly learnt to regard themselves as Greek in nationality, and they fought for the Greeks against the Turks or Italians, although they kept their own customs and their own language. Then you get those who are half assimilated in language and in way of life. Lastly are those who have become fully assimilated. These stages of assimilation are of interest for our understanding of the past.

Map 7 (see page 60) shows our area in the Palaeolithic period.[6] We are dealing with 40,000 B.C. to 10,000 B.C. Here you have the coast as it was then, when the ice cap was so much greater and the sea level was 100 metres lower than it is today. The Gulf of Corinth is land, and Corcyra is part of the mainland. This change produced an enormous amount of low-lying pasture land which balanced the huge area of magnificent pasture in the mountains. It thus became the ideal area for transhumant animals, and for Palaeolithic man, who lived by pursuing transhumant animals. This part of the world was the area most inhabited by Palaeolithic man in the Balkans, perhaps even in Europe, solely because it had this tremendous transhumant potentiality. With the added coastal pastures it was the ideal spot. All the rings on the map are big Palaeolithic settlements. There is flint in the coastal area, the obvious material for tools and weapons, and there are an enormous number of bones of animals, which show that Palaeolithic men were pursuing red deer in particular (the type of deer found in Scotland), fallow deer, wild sheep, goats, chamois, a form of rhinoceros and wild cattle. This area lies principally in Epirus, but it goes on into southern Albania and over into Thessaly, just as the transhumants of Classical times and later went also into those areas for their winter pastures. What was the chief area for Palaeolithic transhumants, is today one of the poorest areas in Europe, Epirus, 'the mainland'.

Now we move on to the next period I want to consider, Middle Neolithic, when you had mainly farmers, agricultural settlements and in a place called Porodin (in the area north of Monastir, near the Monastir gap) a mixed economy and a great many figurines.[7] We are talking of about 6000 to 4000 B.C. The Porodin figurines portray sheep, cattle, a bull with a hole in his back (probably for offerings), snakes, pig, a lynx (after which the area Lyncus is called) and a horse. Now it could be a wild horse. If it is a domesticated horse, it is the earliest example of such a horse in the Balkans. The men of Porodin had the same sort of animals as Palaeolithic man. Porodin itself was very good agricultural land. The remains show that the settlers were an agricultural people who lived in houses. We have a model. It is a house suitable for settled peoples, and the chimney is dedicated evidently to a female goddess.

The Porodin people were one group that came down from the Danube valley with what is called the Starčevo culture. Another group came down the west side of the peninsula. They were pastoral peoples, moving probably as transhumants and already in the middle Neolithic period, there is evidence of transhumant movement between two sites (Cakran and Dunavec) which have exactly the same culture and many animal bones of the right kind. We can see that the western area finally became transhumant with occasional hut-encampments on the plains, made exactly like the modern Vlach hut-encampment or the Sarakatsan encampment, with poles and branches. Such a form of life extended right down into Boeotia and even parts of the Megarid. This happened along-side settled agricultural people. Many people in this period were agriculturalists, who had come from Asia Minor and settled in east Greece, because they found it suitable in climate. So already in the period from *c*. 6000–4000 B.C. you have a pattern which is not unlike that of the fourteenth, fifteenth, sixteenth and seventeenth centuries, when transhumant migrants pushed their way through settled peoples and reached down as far as the Gulf of Corinth.

The next period I want to consider is Middle Helladic.[8] Then a new lot of migrants began to enter the Greek peninsula about 2200 B.C. The first sign of them is the tumulus. Closely resembling in their way of life the Vlach professional transhumants, these migrants came from south Russia and spread into the western Balkans including central Albania around 2200–2100 B.C. They were found also on the island of Leukas. The signs of their presence are tumuli, and only rarely the remains of a hut encamp-ment. The earliest sort of tumuli had a pit in the centre, which is an imitation of a pit dwelling and in that pit the first burial was made. Then you put a ring of stones to mark the circle, and then you put earth on top to cover the circular area. You put other burials in the mounds, and then when you have completed the burials you put stones over the top.

Sometimes we find a double tumulus. The secondary tumulus was built later, at a time when the primary tumulus had been en-closed with earth and stone. Sometimes a secondary tumulus is about forty metres in diameter. There is a group of such tumuli, not all as big as this, in a place called Pazhok, in the centre of Albania. The users of the tumuli had particular rites and cere-monies. They sacrificed animals such as oxen and sheep. The weapons in the graves show that they were a very well-armed people. The tumuli were used over periods of up to 1000 years, evidently by people who always came back to the same place. It is a feature of transhumant pastoralism that you always go back to the same winter and summer pastures. Those who were buried under the tumuli were certainly the leaders of tribes which practised transhumant pastoralism. They were similar, I suggest, to the Vlachs.

Centres with such tumuli extend from Albania into western

Macedonia, which again is a pastoral area, and down the Haliacmon Valley. Towards 2000 B.C. we begin to find tumuli in Greece. They appear at Elatea and Chaeronea first, then they appear at Lerna. Together with them in the Argolid at that time are a lot of huts, of the hut-encampment type, dating to the last phase of Early Helladic. Then in Middle Helladic you get them appearing in the Peloponnese and even in an island like Ceos. Now the peculiar phenomenon is that the tumuli appear at places which soon became the leading centres of Mycenaean civilisation; grave circles (so called) are found at Leukas and at Mycenae, and tumuli at Argos, Lerna, Malthi and Pylos. The most recent of course are at Marathon where four tumuli form a sequence. It is almost impossible to avoid the conclusion, I think, that these migrants were the founders of Mycenaean centres, bringing their own language and customs, as the Albanian migrants did later, and assuming the leadership over the settled peoples. The migrants were called the Kurgan people by Russian archaeologists, because the world for tumulus is *kurgan* in Russian, and they are all marked by this very peculiar method of burial. Before any of these tumuli were found in parts of the Balkans (this happened only in the 1950s), it had been concluded by philologists that the Kurgan peoples were the so-called Indo-Europeans who brought Greek and Illyrian into the Balkans, and archaeological evidence reinforces this conclusion.

These people were the first Greek-speakers in the peninsula on the normal interpretation, and they invented or persuaded others to invent a linear script which recorded their language, an early form of Greek. But they remained throughout the Mycenaean period the dominant race, the citadel holders, the rulers and the warriors. They retained their character right through the Mycenaean period. No doubt they were reinforced from the north; for people like Achilles worshipped the Zeus of Dodona (in Epirus), and they had the form of leadership which is found in pastoral groups. They did not in fact get absorbed into the pre-Greek community because they were of a particularly masterful warrior type.

The decline of Mycenaean civilisation and the breakdown of Mycenaean power which came about after the Trojan war were caused according to Thucydides by internal faction among the leading powers in the mainland. At this time we begin to get evidence of movements out of Epirus.[9] This led eventually to 'the

Dorian Invasion' and to the re-peopling of most of Greece, and particularly the Peloponnese, with alien people, Greek-speaking, but a different breed of Greek. Just before and again after it we see a further spread of tumulus-burial in Epirus (mainly in what is now southern Albania). We find very powerful weapons. Their knives are typical. There are also battleaxes of various kinds, spears with faceted sockets, javelins of small size and a particular form of short sword. There are more battleaxes of various collared types. These are thick on the ground in what is now Albania and Epirus. We find also body armour, shield rims and shield centres in some burials. The leaders were very highly organised and highly equipped. Nave Type II swords were very common and faceted javelins were peculiar to this area. Very long pins with swellings, sometimes three feet long, were worn, as we know from burials. These were to hold a cloak together. Transhumant shepherds still wear very thick woollen cloaks made out of a mixture of goat and sheep wool. Also at this time, 1250–1150 B.C. you get a new phenomenon in the pastoral area of Albania, Macedonia and north Epirus, a new form of pottery. Again you have double and triple vases, a lot of them with knobs and a geometric form of decoration, which is still used by the Sarakatsans, a pastoral group in Greece. This decoration is known as 'the north-western geometric style'. Its very wide distribution probably means that a prosperous period began *c.* 1250 B.C. in that part of the world, based on large scale pastoralism, such as arose in late Turkish times.

Here again we have literary traditions which help us to see what has happened. During the generation before the Trojan War (dated *c.* 1200 B.C.) peoples began to migrate from the north-western area by land and by sea: the Boiotoi into what is now Boeotia and the Dorians into Rhodes and the Dodecanese, while a great number reached the Isthmus of Corinth, but turned back when their champion was killed. The leaders of some of these migrating groups were emigrés from the Mycenaean world, called Heracleidae, 'descendants of Heracles', who had found new territories in south Albania and Epirus. The next waves of migrants *c.* 1140–20 B.C. were decisive. Under the leadership of the Heracleidae they occupied southwest Thessaly, much of east-central Greece, most of the Peloponnese and a number of islands. The whole movement was known as 'the return of the Heracleidae' and as 'the Dorian invasion'. Its origins and its progress were remarkably like those of the Albanian migrants and their Vlach leaders. The assimilation of the migrating peoples who had the advantage of speaking dialects of Greek, namely Doric and northwest-Greek, began in some areas *c.* 800 B.C., but it was not achieved in most areas until the late fourth century B.C., when a standard Greek (the *koine*) came into general use.

NOTES

1. M. Hasluck, *The Unwritten Law in Albania* (Cambridge, 1954) pp. 210–60.
2. Described with maps in N. G. L. Hammond, *Migrations and Invasions in Greece and Adjacent Areas* (New Jersey, 1976) pp. 19–35. *See* Maps 1–6 on pages 54–9 of this book.
3. For references *see* N. G. L. Hammond, *Migrations and Invasions,* pp. 52–63.
4. C. N. Sathas, *Documents inédits relatifs à l'histoire grecque au Moyen Age,* vol. II (Paris, 1890) p. 79.
5. N. G. L. Hammond, *Migrations and Invasions,* pp. 37–46; N. G. L. Hammond, *Epirus* (Oxford, 1967) p. 25; A. J. B. Wace and M. S. Thompson, *The Nomads of the Balkans* (London, 1914). *See also* ch. 5.
6. N. G. L. Hammond, *Migrations and Invasions,* Map 17.
7. Ibid., Map 19 and Plate 56. *See* Map 8 on page 61 of this book.
8. Ibid., Map 21 and Plates 6 and 7. *See* Map 9 on page 62 of this book.
9. Ibid., pp. 129–60 with Plates 9 and 10; *The Cambridge Ancient History,* 3rd edn, vol. II.2 (Cambridge, 1975) pp. 678–712.

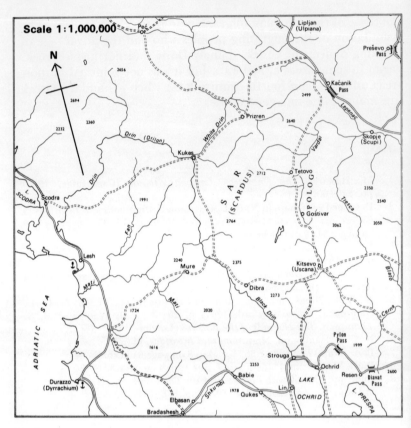

Map 1   Peć to Elbasan

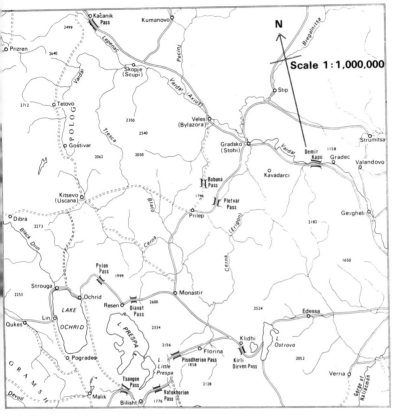

Map 2   Kačanik to Verria

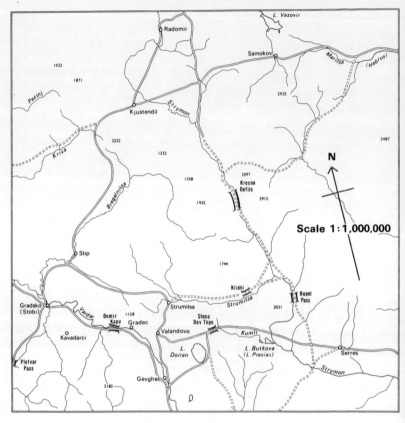

Map 3   Radomir to Serres

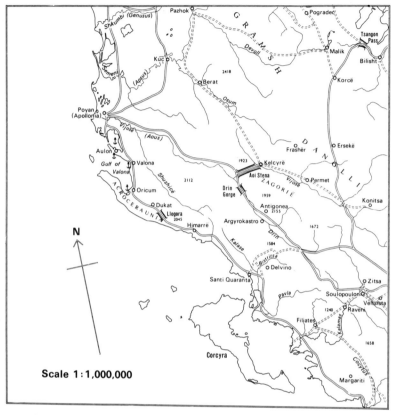

Map 4   Pogradec to Margariti

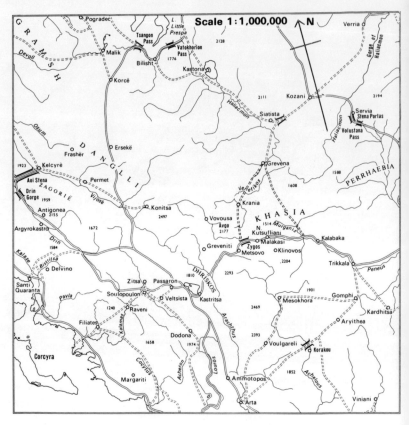

Map 5   Verria to Viniani

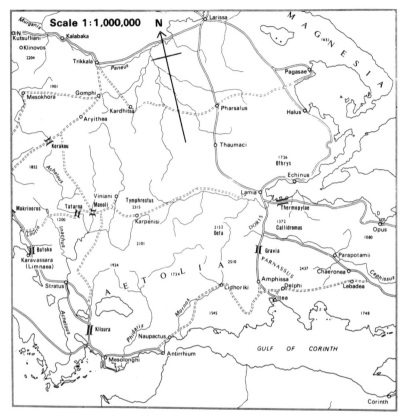

Map 6   Larissa to Corinth

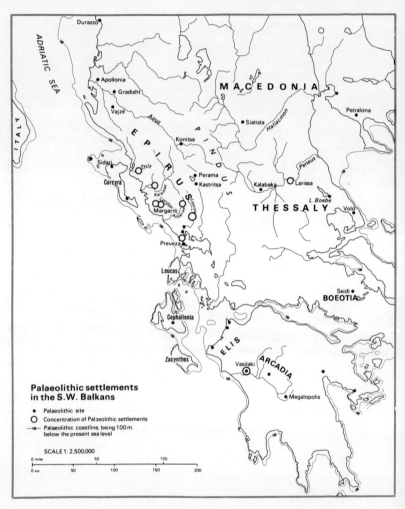

Map 7   Palaeolithic settlements in the southwest Balkans

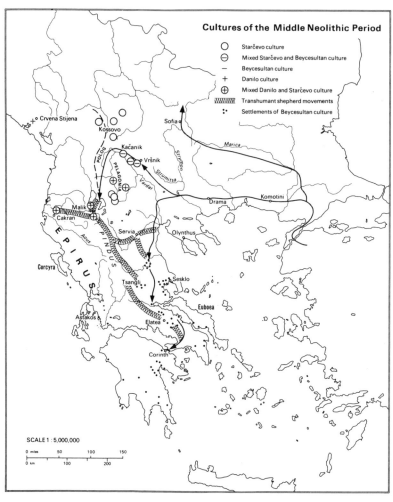

Map 8   Cultures of the Middle Neolithic period

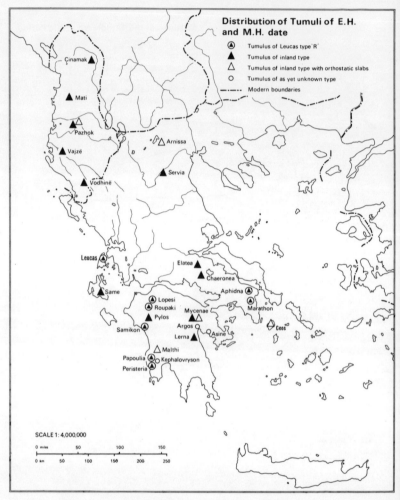

Map 9   Distribution of tumuli of Early Helladic and Middle Helladic date

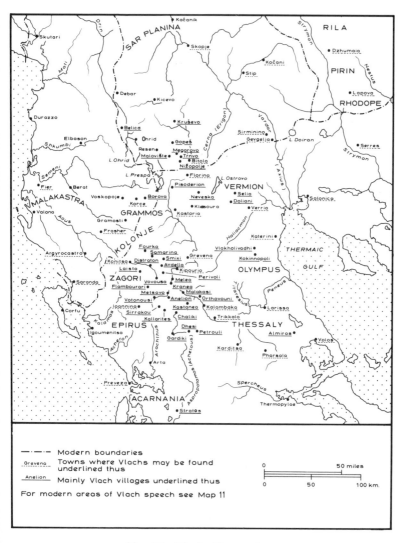

Map 10   Vlach villages today

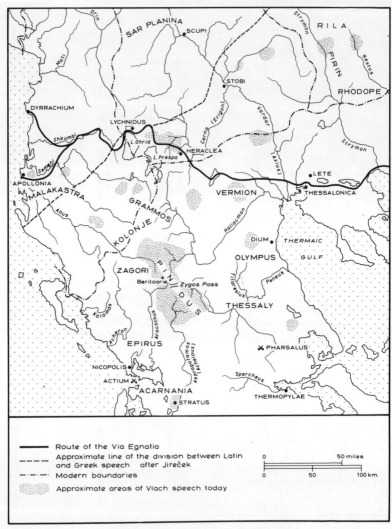

Map 11   The Romans in the Balkans

5 Greeks and Romans

Tom Winnifrith

Many travellers to Greece get no further than Corfu which, in spite of its associations with Alcinous and Thucydides, is with its cricket and greenery and trim tourist villas the least Greek of islands. From Corfu it is two hours by boat to Igoumenitsa and then two hours by bus to the pleasant university town of Ioannina. Most travellers then take the main road which sweeps southward near the site of the battle of Actium past Byron country at Missolonghi to Athens. But there is an alternative route through the Katara pass to Thessaly. In winter and even in spring one can see little on this route except vast tracts of snow, but in summer the red roofs of Metsovo are visible from miles away, and sometimes the bus makes a precipitous detour to Metsovo, bringing nostalgic reminders of Greece as it was before the tourist explosion. From Metsovo it is an hour's walk by mule track or half an hour by a perilous motor road to the village of Anelion. Here one feels that one has arrived in the real Greece that has survived unchanged for three thousand years. The old men still boast like Nestor of their prowess in battles long ago, the young men still strut and sulk like Achilles, the women work and weep and weave their webs like Penelope, and the wayfarer is still greeted with that charming mixture of curiosity and courtesy which greeted Odysseus. As in other villages of Greece the wayfarer must close his eyes to occasional obtrusions from the modern world like the ubiquitous television and signs for Coca Cola. But in Anelion and to a lesser extent in Metsovo he must also close his ears if he wishes to imagine himself transported back to the days of Ancient Greece. For the language they speak in Anelion is not the language of Homer and Demosthenes, it is the language of Vergil and Cicero.

Admittedly this language has undergone a few changes. Some words and even some grammar remain comfortingly the same; *herba* means grass and *fregi* means I broke. A tendency to broaden long vowels, so that 'porta' becomes *poarta* and 'nox' *noapte*, and a tendency to eliminate short vowels, so that 'tace' becomes *tats* means that the language spoken in Anelion has a harsh sound. Not all the changes from Latin have been resolved so elegantly as the useful phrase *are mare nare* which means *habet magnum nasum*, he has a big nose. As in Romanian and indeed other Balkan languages such as Albanian and Bulgarian the inhabitants of Anelion place the article after the noun; thus *barbatslor* means *barbatorum illorum*, of the men. Again as in Romanian one finds vestiges in Anelion of Latin's four conjugations, and indeed the whole grammatical structure of the language spoken in Anelion and other villages is so close to Romanian as to lead scholars of that country to claim the language as a dialect of Romanian. Greek scholars on the other hand point out the large number of Greek words in this language, and they also have shown that the sound changes undergone by these words, sometimes significantly the same as sound changes in words derived from Latin, suggest that these Greek words are not recent borrowings. An impartial philological enquiry might well produce interesting results through investigating which words were derived from Latin and which from Greek. What for instance are we to make of the fact that in Anelion 'I love' is 'agapesku' as would please St Paul, but 'I kiss' is 'bashu', as would please Catullus?

Various names have been given to these Latin speakers, and various derivations invented for these names. They usually call themselves Aromani, and the Romanians call them Macedo-Romanians to distinguish them from the main body of Daco-Romanians north of the river Danube. The Greeks usually refer to the Latin speakers in their land as Koutzovlachs. The word Vlach in Greek means a shepherd, and this is misleading, since not all Vlachs are shepherds any more than all shepherds are Vlachs. Koutzos means lame, and we have here probably an allusion to the hesitant way the Vlachs speak Greek, or even an indication of the sibilant nature of the Vlachs' own tongue. The same is probably true of the Yugoslav name, the cincars, although since cinci (pronounced tsintsi) is the Vlach for five, a fanciful explanation of this term as a reminder that the Vlachs are descendants of the fifth legion has been produced. Some Albanian Vlachs are called

Farsheroti, because they come from the district of Farshër; a more romantic theory, that we have here a reference to the battle of Pharsalus, is untenable. The basic term Vlach which I shall use for Latin speakers in the southern Balkans would seem to be a Germanic word for stranger, borrowed by the Slavs. It is therefore not significant that Wallachia is a province of Romania, or that the Romanians are sometimes known as Wallachians, since the Welsh and the Walloons are evidence of the indiscriminate use of this term. Attempts to derive the name Vlach from the Roman general Valerius Flaccus, or onomatopaeically from the noise of bleating sheep, or from the Roman word for a tenant farmer *fellacus*, from which we get the word 'fellaheen', or from the River Volga, are amusing examples of the eccentric nature of many studies of the Vlachs.

The exact number of Vlachs is hard to determine. Writing in 1894 the great German philologist G. Weigand estimated with Teutonic precision that there were 373,520 speakers of Vlach. In 1914 A. J. Wace and M. S. Thompson, whose book *The Nomads of the Balkans* is still the only study of the Vlachs in English, declared that Weigand had underestimated the size of the average Vlach family, and put their number as high as half a million. The First World War and the Balkan wars that preceded it cannot have helped the Vlach numbers, and in 1918 the Serbian geographer J. Cvijić called the Vlachs 'un peuple qui disparait' and estimated them to be no more than 150,000 strong. Official census figures both from Greece and Yugoslavia are variable and unreliable owing to bilingualism and the reluctance of governments to make much of alien minorities. It is also hard to determine exactly what constitutes a Vlach speaker, since at one end of the scale there are a few old ladies who are monoglot Vlachs, and at the other are people conscientiously trying to learn Vlach in the same way as some people in England in a fit of antiquarian zeal are trying to teach themselves Cornish. My own estimate of the number of people who habitually use Vlach as the language of ordinary conversation is about 50,000, of whom about half are to be found in Greece and the other half in Yugoslavia, Albania and Bulgaria.[1]

The location of the Vlachs is another problem. Linguistic maps, once the favourite toys of Balkan statesmen, are peculiarly unreliable when it comes to delineating the habitat of the Vlachs, since in addition to the bilingualism and nomadic behaviour of many Vlachs, we have the problem that many Vlach settlements are to be found near large tracts of uninhabitable mountain. These factors tend to give the impression of an abundance of Vlachs in the Balkans, and Romanian maps certainly give this impression in contrast to Greek maps in which the Vlachs are not marked in any large numbers. Serbian and Bulgarian maps tend to find more evidence of Vlachs in the country other than their own. Impartial maps like those of Weigand and Wace and Thompson are still remarkably accurate in depicting the main areas of Vlach settlement and provide evidence of the persistence of the Vlachs in retaining their identity. Since the time of these writers, political, educational and economic pressures have depleted the numbers in Vlach villages, but in spite of considerable migrations by other nationalities Vlachs have tended to remain in their own villages, although still retaining something of their nomadic ways.[2]

The main area of Vlach settlement is the central Pindus. Here there are about two dozen villages to the north and south of Metsovo which is in the centre of them. Administratively these villages are in four different *nomoi*, and the fact that the capital of the *nomos* is the centre for local bus journeys makes communication between one Vlach village and another difficult. Thus one can walk from Metsovo to Malakasi and Chaliki in half a day, and the bus journey via Trikkala, if one is fortunate with connections, takes about the same time. Some of these villages are inhabited all the year round, and in others there is a mass migration before the winter to the plains of Thessaly and Epirus. This migration is now conducted by bus, lorry and car instead of the more picturesque mule trains of Wace and Thompson's day, and both in Samarina, where Wace and Thompson stayed, and the southern village of Gardiki I formed the impression that many of the inhabitants regarded their villages as little more than places in which to take summer holidays, although Samarina's inhabitants are very proud of their village. There seems no particular reason why some villages migrate and others do not; thus the two famous villages of Sirrakou and Kallarites on the western slopes of the Pindus are situated in an equally impressive and inaccessible position close to each other, but only Kallarites is inhabited in winter. The villages on Mount Vermion are deserted in winter, but those on Mount Olympus are inhabited all the year round; both these areas would appear to have been settled in the nineteenth century as a result of an exodus from the Grammos massif on the Albanian border, where Vlach settlements would seem to have fallen a victim to international politics. Vlachs are reported near Drama and in mountainous areas along Greece's northern boundary, although here there may be confusion with non-Latin-speaking nomads. To the north of Salonica Weigand noted a tribe of Vlachs speaking a peculiar dialect known as Meglen Vlach. Some of these migrated to Romania, and some being Mohammedans went to Turkey, but apparently there are still Meglen Vlachs in this area north of Ardhea. South of Florina and east of Kastoria there are about five Vlach villages including the once famous and large Vlacho Kleisoura with its grey gaunt houses and commanding position. Many towns near Vlach settlements also contain little colonies of Vlachs, but it is precisely these Vlachs who are most likely to lose their language and identity.

In Yugoslavia Vlachs have shown remarkable tenacity in still living in the same five villages on Mount Pelister which they inhabited in Weigand's time, and there are also Vlachs in Kruševo, now being developed by the Yugoslav government as a ski resort and a somewhat dubious shrine of Macedonian nationalism. In the south east there are many Vlachs near Kočani. Some of these Vlachs and Vlachs who penetrated even further north only to lose their identity in the towns would appear to have moved northwards in the nineteenth century, but the settlements of Malovište and Gopeš claim to be at least six hundred years old. Although Weigand claimed that the Vlach spoken in these two villages had many peculiar characteristics, tape recordings made in Anelion proved intelligible in Malovište and vice versa. In Albania there were considerable migrations of Vlachs to Romania before the Second World War, and political events after the war have hardly helped the Vlachs who used to migrate from the mountains in the east of the country to the coastal plains. On the other hand I did hear of three villages where Vlach was the language of primary instruction, and in the town of Fier on the coastal plain the Vlach quarter was easily recognisable through its cleanliness. In Bulgaria the Vlachs have decreased as a result of population exchanges, but they have survived; for fiscal reasons they are now settled in villages for all the year.

Almost all these Vlach settlements are found south of the line first drawn by the Czech historian Jireček separating the area of Latin influence from the area of Greek speakers.[3] Later scholars have been prepared to modify the Jireček line in places and to admit a certain amount of bilingualism, and the fact that it is the evidence of inscriptions which has been used in drawing the line should be borne in mind. In areas of Vlach settlement few inscriptions have been found or even looked for owing to the difficult nature of the terrain, and the evidence of written inscriptions is not necessarily the evidence of what language was actually spoken. Nevertheless the presence of the Vlachs so far away from other speakers of languages derived from Latin is a puzzle, and regretably the puzzle has not been helped by nationalistic feeling in the Balkans.

For the Romanians anxious to strengthen their claims to the Dobrudja and Transylvania the Vlachs represent a useful bargaining counter if they can be shown to be honorary Romanians, although the links between Vlachs and Romanians must not be too close in case, as the Hungarians maintain, it can be shown that the Romanians are really an offshoot of the Vlachs and only arrived north of the Danube in the Middle Ages. The Romanians on the contrary maintain that the Vlachs migrated southwards in the period between the sixth and tenth centuries, leaving Romania which had been in continuous occupation by Latin speakers since the time of Trajan. Possibly relevant to this dispute is the dispute between Bulgarian and Romanian historians over the origins of the Second Bulgarian Empire, the founders of which are described as Vlachs in almost all our Byzantine sources. For Serbians the presence of Vlachs in Macedonia disputed with Bulgaria is something of an embarrassment, and the few Serbs to write on the Vlachs have tended to consider these Vlachs as late arrivals from further south, whereas Croat historians, anxious to keep the Serbs in their place, point to evidence of a considerable Latin-speaking presence in Serbia in the Middle Ages and earlier. For the Greeks anxious to extend the northern boundaries of Hellenism the Vlachs, usually Greek in religion and culture, and half Greek in language, may fairly be claimed to be Greeks, although some Greek historians have been at unfair pains to eliminate almost completely the Latin element in Vlach language and history.[4]

Vlach shepherds grazing near Beritoarie to the north of Metsovo say that it gets its name from having once been the site of the palace of Olympias, mother of Alexander the Great. Even for one of Olympias' savage temperament the site is too harsh, and Vlach shepherds are unable to explain why Olympias' imperious ways should be immortalised with a Latin name. The alternative legend which is also found in the folk memory of the inhabitants of

Metsovo and in the works of Greek historians of the Vlachs is that Beritoarie is derived from Imperatoria, and signifies the presence of a Roman military camp in the area. Wace and Thompson, though not unsympathetic to the idea of a Roman camp in these parts, are a little sceptical about the name Beritoarie as evidence for this camp, and rightly sceptical of the idea much favoured by Greek historians that the name Pulitsa which is given to the plateau next to Beritoarie should refer to a Greek city rather than be derived from the Slavonic word for a plain, *politsa*. Presumably only an inspired archaeological excavation could establish whether there was a camp here, and, inspired by recent discoveries at Virgina, probe still further to investigate whether there are any traces of Olympias.

Olympias and Philip and their son Alexander the Great are perhaps the most suitable starting point for a discussion of the Vlachs. Not surprisingly, as Macedonia is a bone of contention between various nationalities, the racial origins of the ancient Macedonians are a matter of dispute. It has been claimed that Aristotle was a Bulgarian, and almost as far-fetched are the theories which seek to prove that the Macedonians were somehow Greeker than the Greeks. A more moderate approach would suggest that by the end of the Classical period the influence of Greek from the coastal cities of both Epirus and Macedonia had spread to the aristocracy of most of the semi-barbarian tribes of northern Greece. Some of the rulers of these tribes, and in particular the ruling houses of Macedonia and Epirus, were in any case of Greek descent, and most of the people they ruled spoke a rough and ready kind of Greek.[5] In the years following Alexander's death the rapid spread of the koine based on Attic Greek made the distinction between Greek and Macedonian an academic one.

Epirus, separated from Macedonia by the Pindus mountains, and looking west, whereas Macedonia looked east, led a parallel but independent existence, although Philip's marriage to Olympias gave a temporary unity to the two kingdoms. Other tribes, notably the Lyncestians to the east of Lakes Ohrid and Prespa, were more or less independent for most of Macedonian history, although strong kings like Philip brought them under Macedonian hegemony. The Lyncestian royal house was linked to the royal house of Macedon and like it claimed Greek descent. The Lyncestians and other tribes in this area, though perhaps less civilised than the lowland Macedonians near Pella, would seem to have spoken a kind of Greek, although Philip and Alexander and other strong Macedonian kings did also rule over some non-Greek speakers. The geography of Macedonia, with its large central plain near the coast ringed by mountains, through which there are narrow passes leading to smaller higher plains surrounded by more mountains, transversed by more formidable mountain passes, is such that an uneasy cooperation between lowlanders and highlanders is desirable. The highlanders need the lowland plains for winter pasturage, and the lowlanders need the highlanders to help defend the passes against more formidable barbarians invading from the north.

Two pieces of evidence, one in Arrian, one in Justin, suggest that Philip made considerable efforts to civilise the semi-nomadic highlanders by bringing them down to live in cities on the plain.[6] In both cases the description of the life of the highlanders reminds us of the old-fashioned Vlach, and Philip's civilising mission reminds us of the forces working against the Vlachs' survival. It is not quite clear, however, how far and for how long lowland Macedonia was able to exert such an influence on the highlands. The Macedonian kingdom's boundaries obviously fluctuated between the years 600 and 200 B.C., although the boundary of the present Greek province of Macedonia might be said to represent a base line from which when the Macedonians were strong, as under Antigonus Doson, Philip V's predecessor, they pushed forward to include Yugoslavian and Pirin Macedonia in Bulgaria as well. The Sar Planina, Rila and Pirin mountains are more easily defensible against northern invaders than the present Greek frontiers, where, as in 1941, the Monastir gap is easily passable, but they are of course much further away from the centre of Macedonian power than the line further south, and only reached through difficult mountain passes, where retreating armies are vulnerable. As the Romans found after they made Macedonia a province, and the Byzantines found in the time of Basil the Bulgarslayer, the only really satisfactory frontier for Macedonia is the line which Alexander made its frontier, namely the Danube.

The Danube can, however, never have been the northern boundary of the Greek language. Throughout the four hundred years that preceded the arrival of the Romans in the Balkans the two main contenders with Greek as a lingua franca in the Balkans were Thracian to the north east and Illyrian to the north west. In Yugoslav Macedonia, conveniently and perhaps not entirely coincidentally, there was probably an area of mixed speech; it is not quite clear whether the Paeonians, sometimes replaced by Dardanians, were Thracians or Illyrians. This was the area in which at times of Macedonian strength the boundary of Hellenism was much further north, and at times of Macedonian weakness occasionally and sensationally as with the invasion of the Gauls in 279 B.C., the boundary receded much further south. Celts to the north of the Danube apart from this invasion did not make much impact in the Balkans, although the survival of a Celtic language in Galatia is an interesting insight into the resistance of native dialects to the over-powering strength of Greek. The Scordisci, a considerable obstacle to the Roman conquest of the Balkans, were probably Celtic. Illyrian in the view of most scholars survives in the shape of Albanian to the present day, and Thracian survived until the end of the Roman Empire.[7] The fact that Greek and later Latin were the language of the *literati*, and therefore the only languages likely to be recorded in written inscriptions, has tended to obscure the importance of Thracian and Illyrian, belatedly recognised by philologists in their efforts to explain the substratum of common features in diverse Balkan languages.

The history of Epirus is roughly similar to that of Macedonia. If, as seems likely, the description of Strabo derives from the sixth-century account of Hecataeus, we have a picture of some Greek cities on the south and east, and some semi-Hellenized tribes ruled by kings who claimed descent from Greek houses in the present Greek province of Epirus and that part of Albania which the Greeks claim as their own, northern Epirus. During the four hundred years that preceded the Roman invasion the Epirotes became more Hellenized, and the line of Epirote as opposed to Illyrian influence was pushed back to the future route of the Via Egnatia, although Illyrian invasions were always a threat. Unlike in Macedonia no one royal house ever succeeded in establishing kingship over the whole area, although the Molossian kings, the family of Olympias and Pyrrhus, did create the Epirote alliance, a federal system, in which the Molossians had the largest say. Apart from Pyrrhus the Epirotes were less involved in foreign campaigns, and therefore less likely to suffer the drain on manpower which Alexander's campaigns and the wars of his successors must have in-flicted on the Macedonians. There were of course a few Pyrrhic victories for the Epirotes to suffer, and these may have led to the collapse of the Molossian royal house, the somewhat ignoble and

ambivalent part the Epirotes played in the wars between Rome
and Philip V of Macedon, and then the final débâcle of 168 B.C.
when Aemilius Paullus ruthlessly punished the Molossians for their
support of Perseus against the Romans and the pro-Roman party
in Epirus, by enslaving 150,000 Molossians and leaving the part of
Epirus nearest the Pindus mountains a desert.

Roman involvement in the Balkans began almost by accident in
229 B.C. when, incensed by piratical raids by Illyrians in the
Adriatic, they established a small protectorate in central Albania
to the north of the Epirote Alliance. Within a hundred years they
found themselves in complete control of the difficult province of
Macedonia, although it was then more than a hundred years
before the task of settling the problem of Macedonia's northern
boundary was completed. Thanks to the narratives of Livy and
Polybius we have an admirably full account of the complicated
political and military manoeuvres in the Macedonian wars,
whereas our sources for the history of Macedonia after it had
become a Roman province are regrettably scanty. This is dis-
appointing for the student of the impact of Latin on the Balkan
peninsula, as it is clear that the period after 148 B.C., when Macedonia became a Roman province, is more likely to have brought
about a permanent Latin-speaking population than the campaigns against Philip and Perseus.

Although the topographical details of these campaigns are not
wholly clear it is obvious that the passes over the Pindus mountains
and other ranges in the centre of the Balkans played a great part in
them. In the final struggle against Perseus the Molossians, friendly
to Perseus, held the central passes, enabling Perseus to make his
daring march through difficult country in 169 B.C. to Stratus held
by the Aetolians. The consul for 169, Q. Marcius Philippus, managed to carry the war into Thessaly by dint of taking a southern
route via Ambracia and Athamania, and in the autumn of the
year managed to obtain corn from the Epirotes still loyal to Rome.
This presumably would have come by a northern pass as the Zygos
pass would have been held by the Molossians. The severe punish-
ment of the Molossians which involved the razing of their fortresses
as well as the enslavement of their population would seem to be a
logical if brutal response to the dangers and difficulties which the
Pindus passes represented.

Macedonia was less severely punished than the Molossians, being
divided into four separate republics, although this experiment

did not last very long, as in 149 B.C. there was a revolt by Andriscus, claiming to be the son of Perseus, and in 148 Rome took over control of the province. The four republics survived, and one of them encompassing the north and west of the province seems to have retained some kind of autonomy.[8]

Thus the settlement of 168 B.C. by Aemilius Paullus had a lasting importance for the history of Macedonia, although not as lasting as is maintained by Greek historians of the Vlachs who see in the *praesidia armata*, the armed garrisons, which three of the Macedonian republics were allowed to keep on their frontiers, the ancestors of the armatoles who re-emerge in history some two thousand years later as a semi-independent police force organised by the Turks.[9] The Greek theory is designed to show that the armatoles, many of whom were Vlachs, were in some peculiar way really Greeks, who had picked up their Latin from the Roman military presence nearby. It is true that, though the boundaries of the four republics are a little hard to define owing to the corrupt text of Livy, it would seem that the boundaries of the fourth republic corresponded roughly with areas of present Vlach settlement with the Pindus mountains forming the obvious western boundary.[10] On the other hand, the Greek historians do not sufficiently stress the presence of Roman garrisons in Macedonia. In the settlement of 168, according to Livy, Illyria was free from Roman garrisons, and the same is probably true of Macedonia, although Livy does not say so, but after the revolt of Andriscus a strong Roman presence was certainly necessary, and played its part in defending the province in the difficult hundred years that lay ahead. Indeed, one of the few revealing documents of these hundred years, found at Lete to the north east of Salonica, shows the gratitude of the local inhabitants in 117 B.C. to M. Annius the quaestor; they thank him for not drawing upon the local levies but relying instead upon his own troops and the garrisons in the advance posts to ward off the Scordisci who had already defeated and killed the governor, Sextus Pompeius.[11]

This inscription is of course in Greek, and it is difficult to see why any forerunners of the Vlachs should have changed from speaking Greek to speaking Latin. It is more than likely that quite a high proportion of the wilder districts of both Macedonia and Epirus were still at the time of the Roman conquest speaking a non-Greek language. This is less likely in Epirus where in the time of Strabo the Pindus mountains were grazed by the Peraebi, presumably Greek speakers from Thessaly, but more than likely in the north of territory which Strabo calls free Macedonia. Here Strabo talks of bilingual barbarians, and his use of the present tense suggests he is talking of his own time, rather than referring back to the Classical period of Hecataeus.[12] According to Livy a Dardanian claim to Paeonia was rejected because Aemilius Paullus said that liberty should be given to all who had been under subjection to Perseus. The land refused to the Dardanians, roughly corresponding to Yugoslav Macedonia, is of course the area which, according to the evidence of inscriptions, is bisected between a Latin-speaking and a Greek-speaking population, and since Jireček almost all historians have accepted the existence of such a boundary.

The existence of the Vlachs to the south of the boundary is puzzling. If we reject the Romanian theory of an invasion from the north, and insist that the Vlachs are descendants of a population that has been there since Roman times we must reject the evidence of inscriptions, pointing out that if we had to rely on the evidence of what people wrote as opposed to what they spoke, there would have been no Illyrian and Thracian speakers in Roman times or Vlachs in modern times. In suggesting that there was along the central mountainous spine of the Balkans to the south of the Jireček line a considerable body of non-Greek speakers, who then adopted a kind of Latin, we have no evidence apart from the odd place name and unreliable fragments of oral tradition, which may go back no further than the researches of amateur historians of the last century. On the other hand, though there is no evidence from inscriptions for a Latin presence in the Vlach highlands, Latin inscriptions south of the Jireček line occuring in large cities, like Salonica, there is precious little evidence from inscriptions of a Greek presence either. Nor must it be forgotten that linguistic frontiers, although they appeal to the tidy minds of bureaucrats and historians, do not really exist in fact, especially in areas where illiteracy and bilingualism, not beloved by bureaucrats and historians, are the rule rather than the exception.[13]

In A.D. 1894 when Weigand produced his linguistic map of the Balkans, he showed the area corresponding to ancient Macedonia and Epirus as a confused medley of Greeks, mainly along the coast, Vlachs, mainly in the hills, compact bodies of Turks, Albanians and Bulgars, with occasional eccentricities like Serbs and Pomaks, and dubious entities like Macedonian Slavs completing the patchwork quilt. Today, of course, most nationalities have retreated within their national frontiers, with only the Vlachs stubbornly holding out in the areas Weigand allotted to ti.°m. Two thousand years before Weigand a linguistic cartographer might have observed a similarly confused picture. There would of course have been no Turks, Bulgars, Pomaks, Serbs or Macedonians. The Greeks would have held sway along the coasts, and a little further inland from the boundaries depicted by Weigand, although not so far as the present Greek frontier. Illyrians would have been dominant in most of Albania and Yugoslavia, although Yugoslav Macedonia would have been then, as now, a disputed area. Celtic tribes which were largely confined to the north of the Danube had invaded and would invade along the Vardar and Strymon valleys, and there would be scattered pockets of them in southern Yugoslavia. Bulgaria, the Greek provinces of Thrace and Turkey in Europe would, apart from the coastal districts, be inhabited by Thracian speakers.

The position of Latin speakers is more problematical. On the coast, opposite Brindisi and Otranto, proximity to Italy and the longstanding Roman occupation must have produced a considerable body of people for whom Latin was at any rate a second, if not a first, tongue. The building of the Via Egnatia in the years immediately following the acquisition of Macedonia would have ensured Latin speakers along the western half of this road. Latin colonies were established in cities like Dium, Pella, Philippi and Stobi at the end of the Republic, but, in the same way that Vlachs in big cities soon lose their language, these islands in a sea of Greek are unlikely to have lasted long.[14] Whether Latin speakers existed in the high mountain passes crossing the Pindus mountains is more doubtful. The first Greek to suggest that the Vlachs living in these passes were the linear descendants of Roman soldiers was M. Chrysochoos. His book, though full of a misplaced patriotism in insisting that these Romans were in some way Greeks, does show a keen sense of military strategy. In the Turkish wars of 1884 and 1897, as in the German campaign of 1941, and the Civil War of 1947−8, it was shown again and again that the side which controlled the mountain passes, or more strictly speaking, the heights which controlled these passes, had an immense advantage. After the wars against Perseus and Philip the Romans may have decided to man these passes with a permanent or semi-permanent garrison, the soldiers probably returning, as the Vlachs do today, from the mountains into winter quarters.

In the absence of any archaeological evidence, understandable if the quarters were only occupied in summer, we can merely speculate on just how these camps were organised. As the frontier advanced northwards and as the presence of the Via Egnatia made other southern routes less necessary, it would seem that the presence of garrisons on the passes was less essential. In order to preserve the theory of a permanent Latin presence on the Pindus we must stress the slowness and difficulty of the Roman advance in the Balkans. It is also possible that some of the many tribes who fought against the Romans entered the province of Macedonia as captives and settled or were settled in the least prosperous and inhabited parts of the mountains. The speech of these subdued invaders would in an alien environment reflect the language of those who had subdued them.

The pattern of tribes from the north, entering a Roman province, swearing fealty to the Romans and rapidly adopting Roman speech, is of course a familiar one to students of the late Roman history. There is no evidence for it in the history of Macedonia in the first hundred and fifty years after its conquest, but then there is very little evidence for anything in these years except a bare record of almost continual fighting involving defeats as well as victories, a situation not unlike the story of the last years of the Western Roman Empire.

Cicero, writing towards the end of the first century of Roman rule over Macedonia, said with perhaps pardonable exaggeration that so many barbarian tribes threatened Macedonia that its boundaries were determined by the swords and spears of the Roman soldiers, and that practically every governor either returned to earn a triumph, or perished while defending the province. Unfortunately the poverty of our sources[15] is such that neither the list of those who found Macedonia a quick road to success nor the list of the dead governors of Macedonia can really help us in determining the history of the province in these years. After Andriscus there was a second pretender, followed by a series of raids and invasions from the north. The invaders probably thought that with the collapse of the Macedonian royal house there was little to prevent them from reaching the fertile lands of the south, and their victories over Sextus Pompeius in 119 B.C. and C. Porcius Cato in 114 may have encouraged them in this belief. In 112 Livius Drusus drove the Scordisci back across the Danube and in 109 Minucius Rufus again triumphed over the Scordisci,

although he lost some men on the frozen Danube. In 101/100 B.C.
T. Didius expelled some invaders and added some territory in
the direction of Thrace, but about ten years later C. Sentius
Saturninus suffered some reverses, and Macedonia was devastated. At this period the war against the barbarians of the north
merges with the conflict against Mithridates whose general,
Archelaus, advanced with hosts of barbarians across the Danube.
The victories of Sulla brought no lasting peace, and war with barbarian tribes continued until the Civil War between Caesar and
Pompey. M. Terentius Varro Lucullus, the governor of the province
between 72 and 70 B.C. was fairly successful in pushing back these
tribes, and the Danube as a possible frontier began to seem feas-
ible. Any prosperity that his successful governership might have
brought would appear to have been dissipated by the rapacious
administration of Piso from 57 to 55 B.C. when we hear of
Thracians setting up camps along the Via Egnatia. Unfortunately
Cicero's speech against Piso does not give us a very full account of
the condition of Macedonia, although it would not be rash to
assume that other Latin speakers apart from Piso descended on the
province for their fair share of the spoil. Piso was actually accused
of ill treating Italian merchants in the Balkans, and we do hear of
Romans like Cicero's friend Atticus owning estates across the
Adriatic.[16]

Ironically, one of the few periods in which Macedonia was relatively free from foreign invasion was that in which three major
battles in the Roman Civil Wars were fought on its soil. Perhaps
misled by the example of Sulla who had come from the east to win
the Civil War against the party of Marius, first Pompey, then
Brutus and Cassius, then Antony, went east, only to meet with
defeat at Pharsalus, Philippi and Actium. The idea that the
present Latin speakers in Greece are the descendants of Pompey's
legions is the most romantic, if not the most fantastic, explanation
of the origin of the Vlachs. I have heard Vlachs speculating that
they may be descended from remnants of Antony's army after the
débâcle of Actium, and no doubt there could be found some
northern Vlachs near Philippi or at any rate along the route of the
Via Egnatia, who would argue that their ancestors fought like
Horace for Brutus and Cassius, threw their shield away, but did
not return to make peace and write satire, preferring instead to
retire to the mountains and father Vlachs.

All this is of course pure speculation. Nevertheless the civil wars meant there was a considerable Roman military presence in the Balkans, and one would have thought it would have led to the presence of Latin speakers. Local Greek-speaking soldiers fought in all three campaigns, usually being on the losing side, but the presence of Greeks and Romans in the same army, would surely have meant that the Greek speakers learnt some Latin. We know that some veterans of Pompey left behind in Thessaly fought for Brutus and Cassius.[17] Caesar's march from Dyrrachium to Pharsalus across the Pindus mountains, probably via the Zygos or Katara pass, would seem to have demonstrated the existence and importance of routes south of the Via Egnatia. An army fights on its stomach, and both on this march, the march of Brutus from Athens to Macedonia, the march of his opponents along the Via Egnatia, and especially in the Actium campaign Latin speakers must have communicated with Greek speakers as they demanded food, brutally disputing with Greek speakers in the process.

The depressed condition of Greece is a commonplace among literary authors of the Roman period, and it may be exaggerated.[18] Nevertheless, the strain of three hundred years of war since the time of Alexander, and the diaspora of Greeks over the eastern half of the Mediterranean, would seem to leave something of a vacuum in Greece and Macedonia, and this vacuum could have been filled by Latin speakers. With the victories of M. Licinius Crassus in the Balkans, shortly after Actium, peace was assured for Macedonia, which became an unarmed province, and remained so for the next two hundred and fifty years.[19]

It is at this stage, however, that the difficulties in the way of a permanent Roman presence in the Pindus area really begin. Except in the army where Latin retained its superior status, Greek generally proved the dominant tongue where there was a straight competition between Latin and Greek.[20] Conditions in winter around the Zygos pass are far too difficult to admit of a permanent winter settlement, and any Latin speakers who had manned the passes in summer would have had to retire to the Greek-speaking plains in winter. Although there may have been a track across the Zygos pass that was used in Republican times none of the Imperial itineraries mention any road in this area. Apart from the single place name Beritoarie there is no evidence for any Roman presence. Finally, while the odd Roman legionary or Italian trader may have been able to preserve Latin for a single generation, it is difficult to see how the language could have been preserved for more than one generation without the aid of Latin-speaking women at whose knees the next generation could learn their Latin.

The same objections to any theory that sees present day Vlachs as the descendants of stray Roman legionaries manning vital passes can be levelled against other centres of Vlach settlement apart from the Pindus. The Vlachs on Mount Olympus and Mount Vermion would seem to be comparatively recent arrivals, and they are in an area where in Roman times all the neighbouring people spoke Greek. This is less certain of the people round the passes of Kleisoura and Pisoderion, although we have no evidence of a permanent Roman presence or a Roman road or indeed any settlement before the time of the Ottoman empire. The Vlachs of the Kočani plain, whom Weigand, in spite of evidence to the contrary, assumed to be recent emigrants from the Grammos mountains, might appear to be more likely candidates for the role of representatives of a continuous Roman presence; they lie athwart a Roman road from Serdica to Stobi, and although they are just in the Greek-speaking province of Moesia, and just to the south or east of the Jireček line, they are sufficiently close to Latin speakers at Scupi and to the Danube frontier to make a Latin presence much more likely than in the Pindus.

A Latin presence on the Via Egnatia is much more plausible than in the Pindus. Hammond has established that between Lychnidus (Ohrid) and Heraclea (Bitola) the Via Egnatia must on the evidence of the ancient itineraries and the facts of modern geography follow the modern road through two difficult high passes either side of Resen.[21] It is possible that the two Vlach settlements of Megarovo and Trnovo lie actually on the Via Egnatia, since the modern road at this stage takes a slight detour northwards on lower ground. Of the other villages Malovište and Gopeš, which claim to be ancient foundations, lie to the south and north of the Via Egnatia, while Nižopolje, which lays no claim to antiquity apart from a Roman bridge, is a little further south than Trnovo and Megarovo. Remains of a late Roman fort are also reported at Trnovo and imperial coins have been found at Malovište. Other remains in this area are at Otesevo south of Resen, Ehla west of Resen, Orehovo south east of Nižopolje, Rastani west of Bitola, Velgosti east of Ohrid and Lera slightly to the north of the Via Egnatia. Most of these remains are small and late, and are most naturally taken to be refuges in the period of the late empire. Near Kazani and near Sprci Gorna in between Bitola and Ohrid there are two rather larger foundations, the first consisting of a military camp and a civilian settlement, the second containing a temple and an early Christian church; a bilingual inscription has been found here.[22]

It is practically impossible to reach anywhere between Ohrid and Bitola from the north, unless one takes the three main routes which are now motor roads from Skopje, that via Debar to Ohrid, that via Kičevo to Ohrid, and that via Prilep to Bitola. Thus the stretch between Ohrid and Bitola could not be attacked from the north, but only along the Via Egnatia from the east and west where the high passes near Resen and the low pass near to the west of Bitola are admirably suited to defensive action. There are in addition two good routes southwards from Resen on either side of Lake Prespa as well as the Via Egnatia itself running south-east from Bitola and the road southwards from Ohrid to Korçe in Albania. Thus the two small plains near Resen and further east near the Rotska river south of Mount Pelister are both curiously isolated, and yet obviously important in view of the important road running through them.

In their isolation the plains north of Mount Pelister are reminiscent of the Meglen area which again lies in a small funnel between two major north–south routes, the Vardar gap and the Via Egnatia as it proceeds southeastwards from Bitola to Salonica. But the Meglen Vlachs do not have a main road running through them, nor are there any records of any Roman remains in this area. The need to keep the major route free from enemy attacks must have made a strong garrison necessary. This garrison could have had both winter and summer quarters here. The need to furnish provisions for the troops, to supply food and horses for new troops as they struggled over the passes, and the need to keep the passes would soon attract a civilian population of both sexes. This population, probably composed of non-Greeks, would certainly speak Latin.

The Via Egnatia continued to play a major role in the military affairs of the province until the governorship of Piso when stretches of the road were occupied by Thracian invaders, and even when the garrison in Macedonia was removed to man the provinces of Moesia and Illyricum it would still act as a route to these provinces from Asia and southern Italy. Quite apart from military considerations there would still be likely to be a permanent civilian population. In winter the roads would have to be kept open and travellers escorted over them. The boundaries of the provinces of Illyricum and Macedonia, later of Macedonia and Epirus, lay at different stages of time along different stages of the route. It would be natural for travellers having undergone the rigours of the passes and possible difficulties in crossing a frontier, and having completed half their journey, to want to rest. The proximity of the Bitola plain and the rich lakes of Ohrid and Prespa would supply ample opportunity for trade. Even when there was nothing to do there was always an opportunity for people to graze animals on the summer pasturage of the mountains and bring them down to the plains in the winter. It is as muleteers, tradesmen, guides and herdsmen that Vlachs emerge into history.

This picture of the Ohrid–Bitola road as a hive of entrepreneurial activity by the ancestors of the modern Vlachs in Mount Pelister may seem fanciful. It might receive some support from the variety of different stations in the various itineraries which suggests that the area was well furnished with convenient stopping points, and from the archaeological discoveries in the area. Some of these stations have Latin names, although these may reflect the language of the authors of the itineraries, and some of these names (Castra, Praesidium, Nicaea), suggest a military presence. The preservation of the Latin language from the time when the district was in military hands would be helped by the proximity of the frontier to Latin-speaking Illyricum and the presence of so many Latin-speaking travellers coming from the west. Crossing a provincial frontier may have involved paying customs duties. It is not improbable that there were soldiers in Macedonia even when it was an unarmed province. There is certainly evidence in the late empire for soldiers abandoning their military duties for civilian activities.[23]

Thus though a permanent Latin-speaking population is unlikely in the Pindus it is not impossible along the Via Egnatia even during the first two and a half centuries of the Roman Empire when, for the first and virtually the last time in history, Macedonia was relatively peaceful and prosperous. In the third century the barbarian threat from across the Danube brought into play a number of factors designed to increase the influence of Latin in the Empire. The Danube became the most important part of the Empire, and the soldier emperors of the second half of the third century must have increased the prestige of Balkan Latin in the same way as Justinian, another Latin speaker, brought about a temporary revival of Latin in the fifth century. One of these soldier emperors, Aurelian, by abandoning Dacia increased the number of Latin speakers south of the Danube; although some of the Dacian settlers may have stayed behind, and most of them settled just south of the Danube in two provinces which would shortly be renamed Dacia, some may have wandered further south. More importantly, as the barbarian threats increased Macedonia would begin to need troops as it had done in Republican days. We find an inscription from Ohrid, significantly in Latin, in the time of the Emperor Gallienus (A.D. 253−68), asking for a detachment of two cohorts from the Danube legions. More importantly still, we hear of large numbers of barbarians either roaming around the Balkans as invaders, or being settled as captives, or being bought off by tempting offers of land south of the Danube. As in the west, though these invaders may have retained their native speech for a time, they would soon adopt the language of the country they had invaded, and this language, as is clear from the evidence of Priscus and Procopius, can only have been Latin.[24]

The history of the Balkans between the years A.D. 250 and 500 is fairly obscure. Our sources are often inadequate. The admirable Ammianus Marcellinus unfortunately only covers the middle of the period. Claudian, like Ammianus Marcellinus, a Greek who oddly and perhaps significantly wrote in Latin, has useful information about Greece and Epirus in the time of Alaric, although he is prejudiced and a poet. The reforms of Diocletian, the rise of Christianity, the complicated story of Constantine the Great's success and the romantic adventures of the Emperor Julian have understandably attracted the interest of both modern and ancient historians, but we have far less information about the Gothic invasions which obviously affected the inhabitants of the Balkans more directly. For the important third century, when the Romans won great victories and suffered terrible defeats, apart from fragments of Dexippus who actually took part in the campaigns, we have to rely on the unreliable Historia Augusta and late Byzantine chroniclers. Archaeology can provide some help, but there is much more archaeological evidence for the Danube frontier than further south, and it is difficult to establish a precise and accurately-dated pattern of population movements from the archaeological evidence at our disposal.[25]

Nevertheless, all the evidence we have does point to an increase in Latin. Evacuation of Latin speakers from north of the Danube

1a   View of the Zygos or Katara pass from Metsovo: Vlach women in foreground

1b   View of Malovište, Vlach village in Yugoslavia

2a Gold solidus of Hera-clius (610–41) and Hera-clius Constantine

2b Bronze coin of Küt-büddin *Ilghazi* of Mardin (1176–84)

2c Gold hyperper of John II Komnenos (1118–43)

2d Bronze coin of Nedj-muddin Alpi of Mardin (1152–76)

2e Bronze coin of Husa-muddin 'Yoluk Arslan' of Mardin (1184–1200)

2f Bronze coin of Nasirud-din Mahmud of Kefya (1200–22)

2g Reverse and obverse of 'The Great Ruler of All Romania' (right); and the East, Mehmed (left), the *Melik* Danishmend (1084–1134)

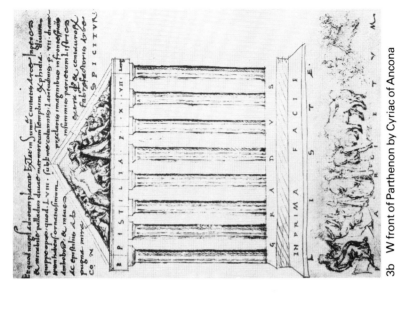

3b W front of Parthenon by Cyriac of Ancona

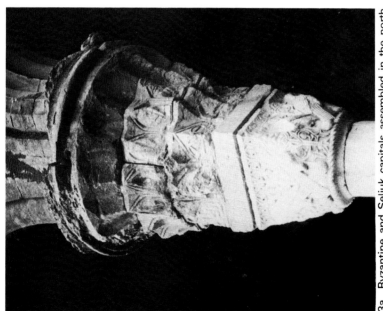

3a Byzantine and Seljuk capitals assembled in the north porch of the church of the Hagia Sophia, Trebizond, in the 1260s

4a   Drawing by Stuart of monument of Lysikrates incorporated in Capuchin monastery, Athens

4b   Etching by Piranesi of Temple of Hera at Paestum

5b Treasury of the Athenians, Delphi

5a Aerial view of Delphi

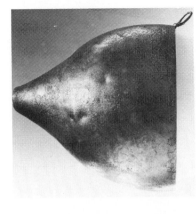

6a Gold death-mask of 'Agamemnon' from Mycenae

6b Attic red-figure bell-krater from wreck of H.M.S. Colossus

6c Oriental bronze helmet

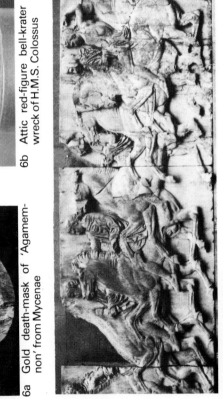

6d Frieze of the Parthenon

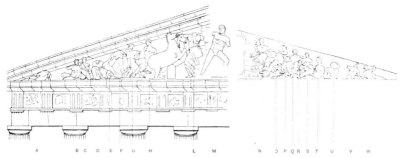

Fig. 2. CARREY'S DRAWING OF THE WEST PEDIMENT OF THE PARTHENON.

7a Drawing by Jacques Carrey of W front of Parthenon

VEDUTA DEL CAST: D'ACROPOLIS DALLA PARTE DI TRAMONTANA.

308

7b 1707 engraving of destruction of Parthenon

8a The Athehian Akropolis

8b Frieze of the Parthenon – Western side

had certainly taken place before Aurelian's decision to abandon Dacia, probably in A.D. 271. Refugees from across the Danube may have been tempted to go further south and east into Thrace and Macedonia by the presence in large numbers in the districts immediately south of the Danube of the very Gothic invaders from whom they were trying to escape. These Goths may either have been relics of successful invasions who, being wounded or weary or willing to make friends with the local inhabitants, stayed behind, or have been settled after defeat in an unsuccessful raid. Even allowing for the unreliability of our sources for the third century, we have plenty of evidence for Goths who were both victorious and vanquished, and in the virtual absence of any survivals of Gothic in Balkan languages we can only assume that these Goths were swallowed up in the general mass of Balkan Latinity.

From the accession of Diocletian in A.D. 285 until the death of Valentinian in 375, though there may have been occasional troubles on the Danube frontier, the middle Balkan provinces of Dacia Mediterranea, Dardania, Moesia Prima and Macedonia enjoyed almost a century of peace and prosperity.[26] As in the previous period of peace that followed the establishment of Roman rule over the Balkans in the reign of Augustus, the peace was prefaced by the complicated civil wars from which Constantine eventually emerged victorious. The tetrarchy which Diocletian tried to establish seems in many ways a long-drawn-out parody of the earlier triumvirate, and the many confusing divisions of the Empire, as well as the battles between the leaders of these divisions, must have further complicated the racial picture in the Balkans. It is perhaps worth noting that, though Constantine, by making Constantinople the centre of his Empire, eventually contributed to the final victory of Greek over Latin as the language of the Eastern Roman Empire, some of the divisions of the empire, in which Macedonia, Greece and all but a small fragment of Thrace had fallen under the rule of a Western Caesar or Augustus, must have helped Latin gain ground at the expense of Greek. The Emperor Constantine's principal impact on the racial pattern of the Balkans resulted from his military reforms. By weakening the *limetani*, troops on the frontier, and strengthening the *comitatenses*, a mobile striking force behind the frontier which could move to any threatened point, he must have helped Latin, always strong on the border and in the army, extend its influence further south. In addition Constantine has been charged with barbarising

the Roman army by admitting German troops, and he certainly
concluded some of his successful Gothic campaigns by admitting
his defeated opponents into the empire as *foederati*.[27]

The Goths remained peaceable until the death of Constantine's
son Constantius, and during this time Ulfilas began converting
them to Christianity. Ulfilas's labours in translating the Bible into
Gothic shows that we must not exaggerate the extent to which the
Goths spoke Latin, although our sources for the life of Ulfilas do lay
stress on his surprising knowledge of Latin as well as Greek, which
would be natural as he was born in Cappadocia, and Gothic, which
would be natural in view of his Gothic blood. Originally Ulfilas
preached north of the Danube, but a persecution of the Christians
by Athanarich led Ulfilas and his flock to flee into Moesia, where
they were allowed to settle. Around A.D. 370 Athanarich was again
responsible for a mass settlement in the Empire of Goths which had
more serious consequences, although his rival Fritigern, who fled
southwards, soon returned. In 376 as a result of Hun pressure Fritigern again asked permission to reside within the Empire, and this
was granted by the Emperor Valens, but the Goths were badly
treated by the *comes* of Thrace, Lupicinus, turned to plunder, and
eventually after a series of Roman defeats there followed the cata-
strophe of Adrianople, in which the Emperor and two thirds of his
army were slain.

At this point the narrative of Ammianus Marcellinus comes to
an end, and it is not at all clear what happened to the Goths left to
roam around the Balkan peninsula. Fritigern's Goths had been
joined by other raiders from across the Danube, and it was a considerable achievement of Theodosius from his base at Salonica to
drive back these raiders who in A.D. 380 penetrated into Greece
and Epirus. The death of Fritigern in the same year left the Goths
without a leader, and they turned northwards. In 382 the Goths
were admitted into the empire to occupy the devastated districts of
Thrace. This won a temporary breathing space for the eastern
empire, and Theodosius was able to turn some of his attention to
the west, although he did try to clear Macedonia, which had suffered terribly after Adrianople from the brigands who infested it,
and settled Goths there.[28] The breathing space was of short duration. In 390 we hear of another Visigothic invasion under the
leadership of Alaric, and in 392 the command against the Goths
was undertaken by the great Vandal leader Stilicho.

The campaigns between Stilicho and Alaric are again obscure.

Twice Stilicho appeared in Greece where the Goths under Alaric were marching unchecked, and twice he failed to engage the enemy in battle. Eventually Alaric and his Goths were allowed to occupy Epirus, from which at the beginning of the fifth century they marched twice against Italy. It would seem that only the tempting prizes in the west saved Epirus from becoming a Visigothic province in the same way as southern France was shortly to become, and it is perhaps interesting to speculate what language Epirus would have spoken in this event. Alaric's death shortly after the sack of Rome in A.D. 410 led to a temporary lull in the danger to the eastern provinces, and the Visigoths settled in southern Gaul.

German tribes were settled in the Balkans in A.D. 427 and 433, and there were serious raids by the Huns a few years later. As with Alaric, so it was with Attila; the temptations of the west and the sudden death of their leader prevented the Huns from making a permanent occupation of the Balkans, although the nomadic existence of the Huns might seem to make a permament occupation a contradiction in terms. Nevertheless after the collapse of the Hun empire in 454 Huns as well as other tribes were settled as *foederati* within the empire. In the reign of Leo (457–74) the Balkans were troubled by two rival bands of Goths, Ostrogoths in Pannonia, and Goths permanently settled in Thrace, both parties being confusingly led by a man called Theodoric. There was also danger from the Vandals under Gaiseric in Africa who raided the coastal areas and captured Nicopolis in southern Epirus. Leo's successor Zeno (474–91) made peace with the Vandals, and tried without a great deal of success to play one Theodric off against another. Eventually Theodoric the Thracian was killed and Theodoric the Ostrogoth after several years of wandering at liberty in the Balkans, either as the Emperor's enemy or ally, moved to Italy in 488. At one stage he and his Goths had been given several cities near Salonica to inhabit.[29]

We hear more about the Goths than about opposition to them, but in the campaign of A.D. 479 there is a clear illustration of the continuing military role of the Via Egnatia and the continuing presence of Latin-speaking troops in the area. As a fragment of Malchus shows us[30] Theodoric the Ostrogoth and Theodimund broke through the passes east of Ohrid, and Theodimund was defeated by the Roman commander Sabinianus somewhere in Albania. Previously another Roman commander Adamantius had tried to negotiate with Theodoric by offering him lands in Dardania. When the Ostrogoths left the Balkans, this particular element in the linguistic melting pot can hardly have been removed entirely. The linguistic map must have been confused, and was shortly to be confused still further, for although the Goths from their new base in Italy made occasional interventions in the Balkans, and there were still Germanic tribes on the middle Danube, the main threats in the sixth century were the Avars, Slavs and Bulgars.

Invasions from these groups were frequent throughout the sixth century, but Justinian still felt strong enough to embark upon his massive campaigns to recover the Empire's western provinces. These conquests were ephemeral, and almost certainly weakened the resistance of the Empire to the Slav and Arab invasions of the next century. Yet Justinian was not totally neglectful of the need to protect his Balkan provinces against the new type of invader. His attempts to garrison the Balkans with a series of forts, though unsuccessful in withstanding the next series of invasions may have done something to help the spread of Latin through the peninsula.

Unfortunately Procopius' account of these forts has not been studied or edited very carefully,[31] and we are not quite sure whether to believe his extravagant praise for Justinian's building achievements in *De Aedificiis* or his sour attack on Justinian's incompetence in *The Secret History*. We also wish that Procopius had been a little less detailed in his location of the Empress Theodora's amatory tastes and a little more detailed in his location of the forts. Imperfect though the narrative of Procopius is, it is clear that the forts were not just on the Danube frontier, but extended southwards to Macedonia, Epirus and even Greece. It is also clear that some of the forts have Latin names. Thus in Macedonia we have Candida, Primana and Placidiana, in Epirus Nova Piscinae, Titiana, Ulivula and Clementiana, and in Epirus Vetus, well to the south of the Jireček line, Marciana, Marmorata and Petroniana.

White though most Vlach villages are in winter and peaceful though they are in summer it would be rash to assume that we can see in names like Candida and Placidiana the forerunners of existing Vlach villages. It would have also been rash of Justinian, particularly after the events of A.D. 479, not to consider the fortification or refortification of the central stretch of the Via Egnatia, and archaeology suggests that he did just this. Further south key passes across the Pindus may have been fortified, although after the Slav invasions it would seem that the principal function of the forts in the south would have been to serve as a point of refuge for the civilian population. In this role, as opposed to their military role of trying to counter any invasion from the north, the forts may have been partly successful and may even have contributed to the survival of Greek, but in their military role the forts proved entirely useless. There were probably not enough men to man them, or enough money to pay the men who did man them.

The Slav conquest of the Balkans was rapid though un-chronicled. In the sixth century we have Latin-speaking emperors, chairs of Latin at Constantinople, Latin bishops, writers and generals. By the middle of the seventh century all that is left of the Latin heritage of Byzantium is the survival of a few formulaic phrases in military commands and imperial ceremonies. This is an indication of the speed with which the Slavs wrested control over that part of the Balkan peninsula which spoke Latin. Nor of course were they stopped by the Jireček line, since they spread throughout Greece, and under Avar leadership threatened Constantinople itself. About the campaigns against Constantinople our Byzantine sources give us plenty of information, and there are a few melancholy and controversial statements about the condition of Greece. But about the invasion of the Latin half of the peninsula we have virtually no information, although archaeology can record the fall of various cities. It is possible that the concentration of our sources on Greece and Constantinople may spring not just from a greater interest in these places, but from the fact that they received the brunt of the Slav attacks, Macedonia merely acting as a transit station.[32]

Certainly isolated groups of Latin speakers in strong strategic situations should have been able to withstand or divert the Slav hordes. The southern slopes of Mount Pelister and the Kočani plain are both ideal sites for such pockets. Snow-covered peaks in July cannot have attracted invaders used to the plains of the Danube and looking for richer plains in the south. The main roads to the south led through Serdica and Stobi, through Lychnidus and Heraclea, but not through the stretches of road that lay between these points. Perhaps, and it is as muleteers that the Vlachs leave history in A.D. 586, and as travellers that they return in 976, a settlement of Latin speakers could be of practical use to the Slavs, guiding them on their way.

It would of course not only be Slavs who would be taking the north–south routes. There would also be Latin speakers fleeing from the thickly populated areas of Latin speakers on the Danube frontier and in Illyricum. The fate of these refugees is unknown. Some clearly fled or were forcibly taken northwards across the Danube, possibly joining fellow Latin speakers who had stayed there since Aurelian's time, although to enter into the origins of the Romanian nation is a difficult undertaking. Some probably stayed in the northern part of Yugoslavia, not losing their Latin speech until after the Ottoman invasion. Others must have moved, or been moved, south. City dwellers, who would have been unlikely to have been able to withstand a harsh life in the mountains, or the rigours of a semi-nomadic life are likely to have gravitated to Salonica and Constantinople, and exchanged their Latin for Greek.

Small settlements of Latin speakers are unlikely to have been able for economic reasons to absorb any large increase in their numbers. Indeed with the collapse of civilisation and the disuse of the east–west roads, as the north–south roads were taken over by the invaders, the main occupation and source of revenue of many Latin speakers along the transverse routes would have disappeared. Indeed with the Via Egnatia out of action all that Latin speakers in key points could have done is direct newcomers on their way south, and perhaps help them found new settlements. Present day Vlachs, or more strictly the grandparents of present day Vlachs, would think nothing of travelling vast distances in search of new homes, employment or summer pasture, and it would not be surprising if the ancestors of the Vlachs in the face of the Slav invasions travelled similar distances.

The Katara or Zygos pass lies two hundred difficult miles south of the Via Egnatia. Continuous Roman occupation is unlikely in this area, although a Justinianic camp, possibly speaking Latin, is not out of the question. The inhabitants of Metsovo in spite of their lack of evidence persist in a belief that there was a branch of the Via Egnatia running through their town, and a Roman camp nearby. It is hard to know whether this merely reflects the views of Greek historians, or is a piece of genuine oral tradition. The former might seem more likely. There is, however, one explanation for the belief that the Via Egnatia went through Metsovo. A party from the old Via Egnatia, perhaps leading a party of refugees from further north, could have led a new colony into the Pindus. Like Helenus in the Aeneid with his second Troy in Buthrotum, and like the refugees from Turkey who have founded many new Smyrnas in Thrace, the refugees from the north could have called the main track through the mountains the Via Egnatia. It is interesting that the main mountain near Metsovo, Mount Peristeri, not only with its combination of bare slopes and well-wooded peaks looks like Mount Pelister, but also has a very similar name. Contacts between the two mountains would be easy to maintain, since the routes are clearly defined. They are the same routes which the Vlachs used when travelling during their great expansion in the eighteenth century.

It is of course impossible to give any clear picture of the linguistic map of the Balkans in the sixth century, and since the Slavonic invasions were soon to alter the kaleidoscope again it might seem unnecessary. It is odd that we can be less confident about the situation at the end of the fifth century than at the beginning of the Roman Empire when, as we have shown, linguistic boundaries were not very different from those in Weigand's day.

Just before the final débâcle of the Slav invasions there is a tragicomic episode, recorded by Theophylact Simocatta and Theophanes, in which one muleteer told another to look to his baggage, and the whole Byzantine army, thinking this was the signal for an about turn, fled in confusion. The episode occurred in A.D. 586 somewhere fairly close to Anchialus on the Black Sea coast, and the words used by the muleteer *torna, torna, fratre* suggest though they do not prove, the existence of Latin speakers in this area. The exact place of the incident is not certain, and it seems surprising to find Latin speakers so far east.[33]

Vlachs, as opposed to possible Latin speakers, are first mentioned in history in the year A.D. 976 when David, the brother of the Bulgarian emperor, Samuel, is said by Cedrenus to have been killed by certain Vlachs between Kastoria and Prespa. Thereafter Byzantine sources mention Vlachs fairly frequently, usually in an uncomplimentary fashion. In spite of the incident involving his brother, there is some possibility that Samuel, variously claimed to be of Bulgarian, Macedonian and Armenian descent, was a Vlach, and certainly the Asenid leaders of the Second Bulgarian Empire are said to be Vlachs.[34] With the break up of Byzantine authority in the Balkans after the Fourth Crusade, Vlachs also appear to have gained for short periods independence in the

Pindus and in Thessaly, which became known as Vlachia. The
Turkish conquest put an end to this independence, although the
Vlachs continued to maintain control of the mountain passes. As
armatoles and klephts they played a prominent part in the early
struggles to achieve independence with little attention being paid
to their Latin origin. This was really only brought up in the latter
half of the nineteenth century when the Vlachs emerge from the
complete obscurity from which I have been endeavouring to rescue
them to the comparative limelight of being a footnote in the
history of Europe.

On the whole, the efforts of Balkan politicians did little service
to Vlachs or their history. The frontiers of the states in which
Vlachs live have survived fairly well since 1918 apart from the
disastrous experiments of Hitler in the Second World War.
Appropriately it was Mussolini who made the last audacious effort
to make the Vlachs' Latin origins a political issue; his attempts to
create a New Roman Empire are hardly an advertisement for re-
writing the present by using the pages of the past. Equally futile
are the attempts by the historians of various Balkan countries to
manipulate Vlach history to fight modern political campaigns. A
new objective study of the Vlachs is long overdue, and should be
undertaken before the Vlachs, having resisted so many enemies
and invaders for so long, finally fall a victim to the corroding
effects of modern civilisation.[35]

NOTES

1. G. Weigand, *Die Aromunen* (Leipzig, 1895) and A. J. B. Wace and M. S.
    Thompson, *The Nomads of the Balkans* (London, 1914) are still among
    the best books on the Vlachs. J. Cvijić, *La Peninsule Balkanique* (Paris,
    1918) is still a good introduction to the Balkans as a whole. Yugoslav
    statistics may be found in F. Singleton, *Yugoslavia* (London, 1975) p. 260
    and Greek statistics in A. Angelopoulos, 'Population distribution of
    Greece today according to language, national consciousness and religion'
    Balkan Studies, xx (1979) 131. The Yugoslav figure for Vlachs (probably
    including some Romanians) in 1971 was over 23,000 and the Greek figure
    for Vlachs in 1951 was 39,855.
2. N. Wilkinson, *Maps and Politics* (Liverpool, 1951) and Map 10 on
    page 63 of this book.
3. For a map of the Jireček line and possible revisions of it *see* A. Rossetti,
    Istoria Limbi Romine, vol. II (Bucarest, 1964) pp. 34–50.
4. The principal Greek writers on the Vlachs are M. Chrysochoos, Βλάχοι χαι
    χουτσόβλαχοι (Athens, 1909); A. Keramopoulos, Τὶ Εἶναι οἱ χουτσοβλαχοι

(Athens, 1939); T. Katsougiannes, Περὶ τῶν Βλάχων τῶν Ελληνικῶν χωρῶν (Salonica, 1964) and A. Lazaros, 'Η Ἀρωμάνικη (Athens, 1976).

5. For the Bulgarian historians Rakowski and Krstović see D. Dakin, *The Greek struggle in Macedonia, 1897–1913* (Salonica, 1966) pp. 12–13. A. Daskalakis, *The Hellenism of the Ancient Macedonians* (Salonica, 1966) is a one-sided, if less fantastic, statement of the Greek view. Hammond and Griffith, *Macedonia*, vol. ii (Oxford, 1979) pp. 39–54 give a balanced account.

6. Justin 8.5[7]–6[2]. Arrian, *Anabasis* 7.9.2.

7. For survivals of native speech see A. Jones, *The Later Roman Empire* (Oxford, 1973) pp. 992–3. Some students of Balkan philology like Weigand see Thracian rather than Illyrian as the base of Albanian which also has a large Latin element.

8. J. Larsen in *An Economic Survey of Ancient Rome*, vol. i (ed.) Tenney Frank (New York, 1975) pp. 443–4.

9. These historians quote Livy 45.29.14 and Diodorus 31.8.9.

10. Hammond, *Macedonia*, vol. i (Oxford, 1972) pp. 73–8.

11. S.I.G. iii. 700. *See* Hammond, *Macedonia*, vol. i, pp. 184–5.

12. Strabo, 7.7.8.

13. What would a modern Jireček have made of the quadrilingual inhabitants of Nižopolje, or the illiterate Vlach I met in Kastoria, who claimed to speak Vlach, Greek, Serbian, Bulgarian, Yiddish, Albanian, German, French, Spanish and Italian. For Latin inscriptions in the Balkans *see* H. Mihaescu, *La Langue Latine dans le Sud-est de l'Europe* (Bucarest–Paris, 1978).

14. P. Brunt, *Italian Manpower 225 b.c.–a.d. 14* (Oxford, 1971) pp. 598–607 for a list of these colonies. By the fourth century Stobi, the most northerly of these colonies, was a purely Greek town with some interesting Jewish features.

15. Cicero, *In Pisonem*, 16.38. There is a useful collection of all the evidence relating to the Romans in Macedonia in Th. Sarikakes, Ρωράιοι ἀρχόντες τῆς ἐπαρχίας Μακεσονιας, Μερος Α' (Salonica, 1971). *See also* Larsen, pp. 422–35.

16. Varro, *De Re Rustica* 2.6. speaks of large estates in Epirus.

17. Plutarch, *Brutus*, 25. Dio, 47.21. *See* Brunt, *Italian Manpower*, pp. 485–6.

18. Larsen *An Economic Survey*, pp. 465–96 and Rostovtzeff, *Social and Economic History of the Roman Empire* (Oxford, 1957) pp. 253–4. Both are sceptical of laments by authors living in the time of the Roman empire to the effect that Greece, and to a lesser extent Macedonia, were mere shadows of their former glory.

19. For this period *see* Th. Sharikakes, Ρωμάιοι ἀρχόντες τῆς ἐπαρχίας Μακεσονίας, Μερος Β' (Salonica, 1977) and R. K. Sheik 'Roman Imperial Troops in Macedonia and Achaea' *American Journal of Philology*, vol. lxxviii (1957) 52–62.

20. For the interesting and fluctuating relationship of Latin and Greek see H. Zilliacus, *Zum Kampf der Weltsprachen im Östromischen Reich* (Helsingfors, 1935) and Jones, *The Later Roman Empire*, pp. 986–91.

21. Hammond, *Macedonia*, vol. i, pp. 37–47.

22. Information gathered from *Tabula Imperii Romani, XXXIV – Naissus Dyrrachion – Scupi – Serdica – Thessalonike* (Ljubljana, 1974). The bridge at Nižopolje I discovered in 1979, and is as far as I know un-recorded.

23. *See* Jones, *The Later Roman Empire*, pp. 429–30 for customs due in pro-vincial borders and pp. 648–9 for the Emperor Leo's edict against soldiers abandoning their duties for civilian life and other instances of unofficial leave.

24. The inscription at Ohrid is discussed by Sheik and Sarikakes, and also by N. Vulic in *Spomenik*, vol. LVIII (1933), no. 176.

25. Yugoslavia and Bulgaria have explored more archaeological sites of the Roman period than Greece, and the Danube frontier has been investi-gated more than other parts of the country. For the difficulties of accurate dating *see* A. Moczy, *Pannonia and Upper Moesia* (London, 1974) p. 300.

26. Moczy, *Pannonia*, p. 296.

27. Zosimus 2.34. Ammianus, 21.10.8.

28. Themistus, *Orationes*, 34.24.

29. Jordanes, *Gotica*, 56.286.

30. Nieburh (ed.) *Corpus Scriptorum Historiae Byzantiae*, part 1, (Bonn, 1829) pp. 250–7.

31. V. Beseliev, *Zur Deutung der Kastellnamen in Prokop's Werk "De Aedificiis"* (Amsterdam, 1970).

32. The Slav invasion of Greece is of course a controversial subject. Most of the primary evidence is cited in the series of articles by P. Charanis, *Studies on the Demography of the Byzantine Empire* (London, 1972). P. Lemerle, 'Invasions et Migrations dans les Balkans' in *Revue Historique*, vol. CCXI (1954) 265–308 is an excellent introduction to both the Slav and Gothic invasions. For a Greek point of view *see* A. N. Stratos, *Byzantium in the Seventh Century*, vol. IV (Amsterdam, 1978).

33. C. De Boor (ed.) *Theophylact* (Leipzig, 1887) p. 100. Theophanes 1. 258.

34. Most of the evidence on early Vlach history is to be found in R. L. Wolff, 'The Second Bulgarian Empire: its origins and history to 1204', *Speculum*, vol. XXIV (1949) 167–206.

35. I am hoping to produce such a study, in preparing which I have already received generous financial support from the British Academy, the University of Warwick and the Ernest Cassell Trust. Maps 10 and 11 (see pages 63 and 64) and Plate 1a and b may prove helpful to any other prospective researcher.

6 Greeks and Turks

Anthony Bryer

Other papers in this book are on Greeks and Romans, Greeks and Byron (and I presume the philhellenes too), and our editors might have added Greeks and Slavs. With friends like these, what do Greeks need Turks for? The difference is that the Turks were something more intimate than friends. Eager suitors, they asked not only for the Greeks' board, but their bed too. So I am dividing my paper into the three stages of intimacy, indeed three of the ages of Man: courtship, marriage, and separation (or its alternative, integration). I am going to emphasise how real and lively that courtship of Greek and Turk was from the twelfth to the fourteenth centuries − the heroic years of the first encounter of the people of Rum with the Seljuks and Türkmans, celebrated in Turkish epic poetry; and of how, among the Greeks and Türkmans at least, came the first warning light of any engagement − the realisation of economic disparity between the two parties. But courtship was followed by a series of marriages, albeit shotgun, in the fourteenth and fifteenth centuries, finally consummated by the Ottomans in 1453. This age is best symbolised by an actual marriage that took place one day in May 1346 at Selymbria on the sea of Marmara: that of the beautiful Theodora, daughter of the Emperor John VI Kantakouzenos, to the ageing Ottoman Sultan Orhan. It was a suitably splendid occasion, with pavilions, song and dance, feasting and wedding presents for the guests to admire, and both families on their best behaviour. I am going to emphasise how real and lively such marriages, and the symbiosis which followed them, could be. But only *could* be, for the Greek guests at Selymbria could not help noticing another warning light. There was something missing at the party that May day. It was not just that the bridegroom does not seem to have turned up (for such weddings are customarily done by proxy), but there was simply no wedding. Theodora kept her faith, there was even a *prokypsis* with trumpets to follow, but no Orthodox wedding ceremony.[1] It was a registry office job: it could be no other. Marrying him is one way to deal with the lodger who won't pay his rent or go away. Convert him to your faith is another. The Greeks had tried both before, with conspicuous success among the Slavs, but to do one without the other is to invite trouble. So finally I am going to suggest how the fourteenth to sixteenth centuries saw a painful process of separation or integration, where if the Greek part in creating (as opposed to servicing) the Ottoman Empire has perhaps been overplayed by those who would like the Greeks to have it both ways, the Ottoman part in defining (and so partly creating) a Greek identity has perhaps been overlooked. It was, after all, the Turk who first established what a Greek was, a legal definition that helped confirm and project a Byzantine (or in their own terms 'Roman'), as opposed to Greek, identity which survived until 1821 when Alexander Hypsilantes found that the Romanians would not rise for the 'Romans', for they (quite rightly) realised that they were in fact being asked to fight for the Greeks. And by making part of his definition that a Greek was a son of a Greek, it was paradoxically the Turk who ensured the survival of those Greeks who did not integrate, with their church, as a separate people in what was now the Turk's own house.

First, the courtship. What were the suitor's credentials? There were, of course, Turks and Turks. The Seljuk Turks who opened the courtship were not the Türkmans who first snatched Greek brides, and the Türkmans were not the Ottoman Turks who took Byzantium. But Greeks were not so good at defining Turks as Turks were Greeks. Ecclesiastics counted them among the sons of Hagar. Chroniclers, with their passion for making even enemies of Byzantium respectable, made them Persians. To intellectuals they were even the sons of Teucer, so that Greeks could fight the Trojan war all over again — keeping it within the family, which did nothing to assuage the loss of the bishopric of Ilion to Sultan Orhan (who was to be one of the family) in the 1330s, while it was not encouraging to recall that Teucer himself had ended up in Cyprus.[2] Armenians like Mathew of Edessa were rather more hysterical: Turks were simply blood-drinkers. It took a Jew to best, and perhaps first, describe the Turks. Benjamin of Tudela is talking of them in the twelfth century. He reported: 'They worship the wind and live in the wilderness. . . . They have no noses. And in lieu thereof they have two small holes, through which they breathe.'³

Let us take Benjamin's three propositions in turn. 'They worship the wind.' They had once been animist; their shamans had venerated the winds and waters, trees and stones of Central Asia. When Alp Arslan led his raid into Byzantine Anatolia at Mantzikert in 1071 (an unauthorised sideshow which led to the collapse of most of the peninsula into his hands without his asking or expecting it), it was only a century since the Seljuks had strayed into the Shia orbit of the decrepit Sunni caliphate at Baghdad and become its guardians. And it was only sixteen years before Mantzikert that the Seljuks had taken Baghdad, as if the Swiss Guard had captured both the Vatican and Rome. So how Muslim were the Seljuks in 1071? It is a question which is near impossible to answer, but it is certain that many Christians and Turks of Anatolia were converted to Islam within a generation or two of each other. But whether the new rulers of the land of Rum, by their own definition a Christian or Roman land, regarded themselves even officially as crusaders for Islam until well into the twelfth century, is doubtful. In the decades after Mantzikert Alexios I Komnenos apparently had hopes of converting the Seljuks, as the Slavs had been before, and making them proper 'Romans'. And in Türkman heroic poetry Greek and Turk fight like clean-limbed heroes, without an ideological thought in their noble but thick heads. And what sort of Islam were they converted to? Between the official Christian Orthodoxy of Constantinople and the official Islamic Orthodoxy of Baghdad lay a great no-man's land of local cults and practices, many demonstrably pre-Christian, let alone pre-Islamic, which linked the two official faiths. Constantinople had been represented by hectoring Greek bishops in cathedrals; now the cathedrals were official mosques, their lands made *vakif*. But in the country the unofficial holy man was eventually to be replaced by the unofficial dervish, and it was in a Christian monastery that Djelal al-Din Rumi first recited his beguiling message of salvation for peoples of all faiths. Even in the cathedral mosque of Aleppo it was the *trisagion* that the *muezzin* sang, for fear that his minaret would fall down beneath him.⁴ Many Anatolian Christians were not Greek at all, but Armenian, already alienated from the Greeks and their church. And on the whole it was the local Armenian church that survived better than the distant Greek imperial'one, when confiscation of their lands, rather than Islamic missionary zeal, put them to the test. But again, what sort of Islam? The Turks had not forgotten the practices of their recent pre-Islamic past. Some of these habits genuinely shocked Greeks until the fifteenth century: mutilation of enemy corpses, human sacrifice (last performed on a grand scale by Sultan Murad II and certainly not tolerated by official Islam), and even rumours of cannibalism. In turn they found in Anatolia practices familiar to them: animal sacrifice in churches, the cult of sacred places and the wonder-working dead.[5]

'They live in the wilderness.' It was this, rather than differences of faith, that flashed the first warning light in the courtship. It was not so much the Seljuks who lived in the wilderness. They had left the wilderness of Central Asia two centuries before Mantzikert, and in fact the new centralised state they established in central Anatolia some decades after 1071 was to be both Turkish urban and Greek agricultural, rather than basically pastoral. Let us forget those Seljuk goats nibbling away the Greek olive groves of central Anatolia. You cook in animal fat, not olive oil in central Anatolia and it was the Turks, not the Byzantines who introduced Classical, not Byzantine, Roman methods of dry farming there; albeit it was the Greeks who dug the water courses for them; while it had been the Byzantines who had bred the Angora goat, whose fine wool was known to Bede long before the Turks came. But the Türkmans who came close on the heels of the Seljuks were a different matter. They brought, or created, a wilderness with them. They were nomadic or pastoralist Turks who interposed themselves in the high summer pastures between the coastal Byzantine agriculturalists and the Seljuks of the centre, an indifferent menace to the economy of both. As late as the 1520s over sixteen per cent of the population of Anatolia was registered as nomad, an intolerable proportion for any agricultural economy, and it was the last, internal, conquest of the Ottoman Empire in the seventeenth century to settle them.[6] These Türkmans rejected the official teaching of the cathedral or mosques. They were Alevi, a twilight Islam from which they could slip in and out of local or crypto-Christian cults. They were the instruments of change, which was economic before it was ethnic. Yet it was also the Türkmans who were among the Greeks' keenest suitors.

To the settled Seljuks of Konya the Greeks offered a formidable list of agricultural loan words, like the *doghan* (*dokani*), the familiar Greek *tribulum* or threshing sledge; the *firin* (*fourno*, *furnus*), or fixed oven; and even, I suspect, the humble dung cake, although it is difficult to imagine a Turk without his dung cake. It was essential to warming an Anatolian winter, unless it asphyxiated one, as it may have done the Emperor Julian near Ankara on the night of 17 February 364. The Turkish word for dung cake is *tezek*, a word first attested by a disdainful tenth-century Byzantine bishop as *zarzakon*, before the Greeks had met the Turks. The word certainly has no connection with the Mongol word for the stuff, which is *argols*.[7] But Benjamin of Tudela's third proposition, that 'They have no noses' is surely a reference to the Turks' Mongol cousins of the past. If nothing else, the marriage of Greek and Turk gave the Turk his nose.

Between Mantzikert in 1071 and Köse Dagh, when the Seljuk state went down to the Mongols in 1243, the Seljuks exposed historic Anatolian boundaries, economic, ethnic, geographical, climatic, which had only been masked by common rule from Rome or Constantinople since Antiquity. The Konya and Constantinople states were centralised, but their resemblance almost ends there. It is tempting to list superficialities, the Seljuk staff of Greek *notarans*, some chancery and ceremonial practice, the survival or adoption of baptism to be on the safe side, Armenian decorators, land grants that look like *pronoias*, *udj-beys* that look like *akritai*; but the Seljuk state was even less Byzantium in disguise than was the Ottoman. The Komnenoi and Seljuk sultans had a healthy mutual respect and even cooperation against mutual foes: the Türkmans and (as they were to suspect) busybody crusaders. Both competed for manpower and it was often the Seljuks who could offer the Anatolian farmer greater security against the Türkman than could the Byzantines. Add to that tax exemptions, and Kilidj Arslan was able to lure Greek farmers, 5000 at a time, over the border to settle in Akshehir. In 1142 John II Komnenos found that the Greeks of Seljuk Beyshehir did not want him. Choniates reports that

Their intercourse with the Turks of Konya had resulted not only in firm mutual friendship, but in the adoption by the Christians of the Turkish way of life in many respects, and they were so friendly with their Turkish neighbours that they regarded the

Byzantines as their enemies. Habit, engrained by the passage of
Time, is indeed stronger than race or religion. The truth was
that in the Byzantine world, by our day, the springs of Christian
virtue had dried up, the truths of religion had ceased to be taken
seriously, and arbitrary injustice had run riot until the natural
affections of the majority of the population had been chilled to a
degree at which entire Hellenic communities voluntarily opted
for finding new homes among the barbarians and rejoiced to get
away from their native land.[8]

The Anatolian peasant had found his home with the Turk
largely before the intellectuals of Constantinople could tell him
that he was in fact Greek. For an identity was now being forced
upon the twelfth-century Byzantine intelligentsia. All had been
agreed that the term 'Roman' meant Orthodox, but it was becoming increasingly clear that Byzantinised Slavs and Byzantinised
Armenians did not want to be 'Roman', and the twelfth century
brought confirmation that 'Roman' certainly did not mean
Roman Catholic either. Patriarch Michael III of Anchialos
(1170−78) announced:

> Let the Muslim be my master in outward things, rather than the
> Latin dominate me in matters of the spirit. For if I am subject to
> the Muslim, at least he will not force me to share his faith. But if
> I have to be under the Frankish rule and united with the Roman
> church, I may have to separate myself from my God.[9]

By elimination, it was becoming apparent to the intellectuals of
Constantinople that 'Roman' meant what we now call Greek, but
by then the Anatolian peasant was already Muslim − of sorts.
So it was 'Romans', rather than Greeks whom the Turks first
courted. They dislocated Anatolians' sense of identity, but in so
doing, located their own. For the twelfth-century Anatolian
'Roman's' sense of *patrida*, his patriotism, was focused not on
a universal non-sectarian empire run by the churchmen and
colonels of Constantinople, but on what the Turks call *memleket*,
a town and its locality, a birthplace the waters and water-melons of
which are sweeter than anywhere else in the world, a sense of locality inherited by the hitherto wandering Turk. But so many Byzantine localities derived their identity from their patron saint, a
ghostly network which had given coherence to Byzantine local

society: Nicholas of Myra, the archangel of Chonai, the Wonder-worker of Neocaesarea, Phokas of Sinope, the Forty of Sebasteia, the Tyro of Euchaita, Tryphon of Nicaea, Demetrios of Thessaloniki, John of Ephesos, Eustratios of Arauraka and Eugenios of Trebizond. Such saints were employers of peasants, priests, monks and merchants, supernatural defenders, hosts to pilgrims, presidents of annual *panegyreis* on their feast days, which tactfully came either immediately after the harvest or before the spring sowing. They were also shrewd businessmen. Part of the Seljuk and Türkman success in breaking local economies and sense of Orthodox *patrida* in Anatolia comes from the way in which they extinguished these local shrines and their lands, for once a pilgrim town has been wrecked it is very difficult to revive. Pre-Ottoman Turkish feelings about such awesome and alien places are summed up in the *Melikdanishmendnâme*. Among Christian heroes of that epic is one 'Metropid' (a fighting metropolitan bishop) and his son Gavras. The Türkman hero is the *Melik* Danishmend. The point of contention is Neocaesarea. And so far as epic tradition went, the key to Neocaesarea was the steep fortified shrine of its patron and evangelist, Gregory the Wonderworker. A Christian Amazon (Amazons are traditionally endemic to the area and we will meet another soon) called Efromiya is courted by the *Melik* and turns Turk. Attractively disguised as a monk, she lures Gavras, captures the shrine of the Wonderworker, and lets the *Melik* in to both the shrine and her favours. The Turks did not pick upon such places (and indeed brides) because they were Christian, but because they mattered.[10]

Gavras, who appears in the *Melikdanishmendnâme*, was representative of a Byzantine who mattered, and survived. He is the epitome of this period of courtship and symbiosis. His very name is probably derived from the Syrian and Aramaic formula g–v–r, 'hero', or simply 'man' — hence Gabriel, 'man of God'. He is a man of one faith in the land of another, a *gavur* or *kafir*, which are the same name. Since 979 the Gabras family had struggled against Constantinople and intrigued with emirs. But in 1098 Theodore Gabras, Byzantine governor of Chaldia, died fighting as a martyr to the Turks at Erzurum. The Greek church celebrates the feast of St Theodore Gabras every 2 October to this day. Of the next three generations of the Gabras family, seven held high office in Byzantine or Turkish courts: two fought for the Greeks; two fought for the Turks; and three fought for the Greeks *and* Turks. The

estates and local authority of St Theodore Gabras, martyr to the
Turks, passed through normal family inheritance to his grandson,
Ikhtiyar ad-Din Hasan ben Gabras, vizir to the Seljuk Sultan Kilidj
Arslan II, from whom it was the Türkmans who filched them in
1192, a century later. At least one Gabras at the Byzantine court
was Muslim; at least one Gabras at the Seljuk court was Christian:
he was John Gabras whom Sultan Kaykubad made his envoy to the
Pope, and Emperor Frederick II in 1234.[11]

The first stage of courtship may be most conveniently illustrated
in coins. I have chosen examples from the Whitting Collection of
the Barber Institute's Coin Collections in the University of Birmingham. Their attraction is that they are humble but essential
things, expressions of state but translatable into water-melons in
the market place. They were issued by twelfth-century Turkish
rulers for their still largely Greek subjects. Faced with the realities
of commerce and custom, most Islamic pretensions go by the
board. They are symbols of a real symbiosis of Greek and Turk.
Among the most striking coins evidently still known in Anatolia
were those of the Attalids of Pergamon, and of the family groups
of Heraclius (A.D. 610–41) and Heraclius Constantine (see Plate
2a). Kütbüddin *Ilghazi* of Mardin (A.D. 1176–84) copied the latter
(see Plate 2b). A more recent Byzantine gold coin depicted John II
Komnenos (A.D. 1118–43) crowned by the Virgin (see Plate 2c),
which was duly copied in bronze by Nedjmüddin Alpi of Mardin
(1152–76, see Plate 2d). The double-headed eagle appears on the
walls of Konya and on coins such as of Nasirüddin Mahmud of
Kefya (A.D. 1200–22, see Plate 2f) before it spreads its wings on the
Chifte Minare of Erzurum (A.D. 1253), and apparently before it
became the symbol of the Palaiologoi and of later European and
Russian empires which came to grief. Another Ortokid coin, of
Yoluk Arslan (the 'Bald Lion') of Mardin (A.D. 1184–1200), who
helped defeat the Crusaders at Hattin in A.D. 1187, has been
claimed to depict the Three Kings and the Nativity, perhaps from
an Armenian illumination (see Plate 2e). The moneyers of the
Melik Danishmend (A.D. 1084–1134) saw nothing strange in
issuing a bronze coinage with his title *Ghazi* (or fighter for Islam)
in Greek, but with the familiar Byzantine bust of Christ. The
examples in Plate 2g simply names him: Ο Μ($\acute{\epsilon}\gamma\alpha\varsigma$) ΜΗΛΗΚΙΣ
ΠΑCΗC ΡΩΜΑΝΙΑC/ΚΑΙ ΑΝΑΤΟΛΗC ΜΑΧΑΜΑΤΗC: 'The Great
Ruler of All Romania and the East, Mehmed'. Perhaps the most
striking demonstration of the symbiosis lies in a still unpublished

Turkish miniature of the Virgin in the Topkapi Saray, Istanbul: Byzantine in iconography, its style belongs to Central Asia. But this period of courtship can be summed up in a single column and its capitals in the west porch of the Hagia Sophia, Trebizond (see Plate 3a). The column is antique; its first capital, of adorsed eagles, whose brothers stand, also re-used in San Marco, Venice, probably belongs to the sixth century. But it carries in turn a 'stalactite' capital of pure Seljuk craftsmanship. The work was assembled in the 1260s, at a time when the wife of an emir of Sivas came pursued by demons to seek comfort at the tomb of St. Athanasios the Demoncrusher in Trebizond. But by then the courtship was nearly over.[12]

Now to the second stage: marriage. I select an actual marriage, that rather laconically announced in a Greek chronicle under August 1352, between Maria, sister of the Grand Komnenos Alexios III of Trebizond, and the Türkman chief of the White Sheep. In a way it is more important than the marriage between Theodora Kantakouzene and Sultan Orhan six years before, because it was the first alliance between a Greek princess and a Türkman pastoralist. The nomads at least recognised its significance, for it profoundly affected the Oghuz imagination. They sang of it in their cycle of epic ballads of *Dede Korkut*. *Han* Turali of the White Sheep tribe wanted a bride. Only an Amazon would do. The *tekfur* of Trebizond had such a bride, but that meant descending from the freedom of the open pastures of the Türkmans through the dark valleys of the Pontos with its *agach denizi* (sea of trees), where armed men lurked, to the alien and enclosed world of the coastal Greeks: a world fraught with danger. For a pastoralist the journey to the coast was traumatic. *Han* Turali's father warned him against it:

> Son, in the place where you would go,
> Twisted and tortuous will the roads be;
> Swamps there will be, where the horsemen will sink and never
>   emerge;
> Forests there will be, where the red serpent can find no path;
> Fortresses there will be, that rub shoulders with the sky . . .
> Your destination is a frightful place. Turn back!

Han Turali, nothing daunted, got to his frightful destination, Trebizond. Here in the *maydan* square he had to undergo three labours which would have daunted Hercules, before he could snatch his bride: to down a black bull, a royal lion and a vicious camel. When *Han* Turali unveiled himself, however, the Trapezuntine *despoina hatun* had other ideas: she

> was watching from the palace and went weak at the knees, her cat miaowed, she slavered like a sick calf. To the maidens at her side she said, 'If only God Most High would put mercy into my father's heart, if only he would fix a brideprice and give me to this man! Alas that such a man should perish at the hands of monsters!'

Turali disemboweled the bull; there were alarming scenes in the *maydan* when they brought on the lion, who 'roared, and every single horse in the square pissed blood', and the Trapezuntines tried to nobble the camel. Turali won his Amazon girl; the first Türkman to claim a real Greek princess. They rode off. But the *tekfur* of Trebizond repented his loss and sent his army to retrieve his daughter. She took matters in hand and sliced up 600 Trapezuntine warriors. Turali's manhood was slighted; they duelled and the princess shot a headless arrow 'that sent the lice in Turali's hair scuttling down to his feet'. They were reconciled and *Han* Turali and his Greek princess lived happily ever after. So says the ballad. History says that they were married for at least fifteen years, that Maria the Amazon kept her faith in the tents of the sons of Hagar and that Alexios III and the White Sheep chief exchanged four state visits from city to pasture. The diplomacy worked so well that ten further princesses of Trebizond were sent to marry Muslim rulers.[13]

But what happened when Greek married Turk? Greeks might regard it as the establishment of a sort of permanent High Commission in a Muslim court, protectress of local Christians. But Turks thought of it more as an expression of vassalage: they had other wives too. Then, Greek and Turkish practice is directly opposed in custom: Greek brides bring a dowry, but Turks buy their wives with a bride price. In practice both seem to have been paid. And then there is the little question of the wedding itself. *Han* Turali and Maria had none: in true epic tradition the hero had snatched his bride, as Digenis or David of Sassoun had done before him. But the heroic period of courtship was over by the late fourteenth century. There was the reckoning to be made in the cold light of day the morning after the wedding. That marriage between Theodora and Orhan at Selymbria in 1346 might have been a fine sight, but Doukas, who wrote in Greek, who was Latin by faith, and whose grandfather had gone over to the Turks, was appalled. The bridegroom sultan

> was like a bull which had been parched by the burning heat of summer, and was with mouth agape drinking at a hole filled with the coolest water, but unable to get his fill. The Turks are intemperate and lustful as no other people, incontinent beyond all races and insatiate in licentiousness. It is so inflamed by passion that it never ceases unscrupulously and dissolutely from having intercourse by both natural and unnatural means with females, males and dumb animals. If the people of this shameless and savage nation seize a Greek woman . . . they embrace her as an Aphrodite . . ., but a woman of their own nation . . . they loathe as if she were a bear or a hyena.[14]

I quote this sort of reaction, which is conventionally worded, because it becomes increasingly and inescapably commonplace in the last century of Byzantium. Doukas has no comment on the Byzantine princess Simonis who was married at the age of five to the formidable and thrice-married Tsar Milutin of Serbia. But that was an Orthodox marriage.

Things had changed since the twelfth century. For the peasantry of Anatolia, the transference of their faith and popular culture may not have been a painful thing. 'Habit, engrained by the passage of Time is indeed stronger than race or religion.'[15] But from the mid fourteenth century the new Ottomans were facing Constantinople itself: the religion of its patriarchate, the rediscovery of their Greek race by its intelligentsia. At the end of the fourteenth century an Islamic revivalist, Sheikh Bedreddin, preached the Gospel of Barnabas among the Christian subjects of the Sultan, a synthesis of Islam and Christianity. But anyone who has the slightest doubt about the authenticity of the Book of Mormon will have no difficulty in dismissing the Gospel of Barnabas. The faiths could not be related. It was quite simply the question of the Incarnation of Christ: there is no reconciliation. The marriage was void. St Gregory Palamas knew it. In 1354 Palamas, in Turkish captivity, met another group of people who were trying to bridge the faiths: the Chiones. They seem to have been Greeks who had embraced Judaism in the hope that it was a halfway house to Islam and that they would get the best of both worlds. But, as Palamas pointed out, they were taking a step back, not forward, in the three Islamic stages of revelation. The Chiones were mortified to find both the archbishop and the mullah of Nicaea condemning them.[16] The emperor, Manuel II, knew it. Dragged unwillingly on campaign as vassal of Sultan Bayezid in 1391, against the Türkmans, he wrote tortured letters back to his prime minister, Demetrios Kydones, of the enforced joviality of the strenuous drinking bouts in the sultan's tent and of how they had marched through the ruins of once-Byzantine cities: 'We destroyed these places and time has destroyed their name'. He endured a winter in Ankara arguing about the two faiths with Islamic theologians.[17] There was no point of contact: the Incarnation stood between them. The marriage was void.

Not that actual marriages were unproductive: after Orhan had set the style in 1346, no Ottoman sultan married one of his own people − or indeed actually married. In 1453 Mehmed the Conqueror was perhaps one sixteenth Turkish by blood. He had a very decent hereditary claim to the Byzantine throne and an even better one to the Serbian. The House of Osman had become, quite literally, the last Byzantine dynasty. But it was Muslim, and in Ibn Khaldun's words: 'The common people follow the religion of the ruler.'[18]

But what was the religion of the last emperors? Demetrios Kydones, Manuel's prime minister, was a Roman Catholic, yet by his opposition to the Turk demonstrated that it was still possible to be a Greek (or rather Hellene, a term he uses in the ethnic sense). Doukas, whom I have been quoting, was an employee of the Genoese in the Aegean as envoy to the Turks. Yet when Constantinople fell he declared himself a Hellene. The last emperor was in communion with Rome, and the last mass in Hagia Sophia was a Uniate one, yet Constantine the Last, too, had decided he was a Hellene.

Of 1453 one must make three points. First, the Fall of Constantinople came only just in time to save the Greeks. Before 1453 the Orthodox Church, and the Greeks as a people, had not been recognised as distinct. After 1453 the Conqueror defined what a Greek was: he was a 'Roman' (*Rumi*) and a member of the Orthodox Church and so of a protected *millet*. Hence those areas which had fallen before 1453 (most of Anatolia, especially) were lost; but those areas conquered after 1453, like the Pontos and much of what is now Greece, could more or less survive as Greek. It was a matter of separation, *apartheid*, as opposed to the integration of the heroic days of courtship to an unequal marriage.

Second, in 1453 Mehmed II decapitated the Byzantine *Hochkultur*. There was only the *Volkskultur*, a Greek popular culture left, and we have seen how that merged in Anatolia with what is now Turkish popular culture. But the peculiar characteristics of Byzantium as Byzantium had been dependent upon a small metropolitan intelligentsia who had in these last years been defining their Greekness. Their loss was a bodyblow, and the Phanariots of the patriarchate were only a musty substitute.[19]

Third, even in 1453 Mehmed II still had too few Turks, or rather Turkified Muslims, to go round. His solution was to secure his towns as Turkish, as the Seljuks had before: Muslim islands in Greek seas. How this actually happened may be demonstrated once more by the case of Trebizond, which he captured in 1461. He began to break the Greek monopoly of the place by deporting them to Istanbul and elsewhere, and replacing them with Turks, or more probably recently-converted Christians, soon after the conquest. The consequence was that by 1486 Trabzon was about nineteen per cent Muslim. But even with forcible deportation (*sürgün*) people tended to drift back home, while Muslims were clearly not at home in what was still essentially an infidel city, with only one converted church as a mosque. So by 1523 the Greek population, at about sixty-nine per cent, was overtaking the Muslim (at about fourteen per cent) and within a few years was in danger of making the place entirely Christian again. So there was a second *sürgün* which reversed the Christian–Muslim population to fifty-three–forty-seven per cent in 1553 and forty-six–fifty-four per cent in 1583. Once the fifty per cent balance is tipped, whole communities go over in a landslide, for parishes paid a fixed levy which had to be carried by fewer and fewer. And, of course, recent converts tried harder and were in fact responsible for all but one of the city's older mosques. But there is another factor. Circumcision does not endow one with Turkish speech or thought overnight.[20] The citizens of the town were the same, speaking (and dare one say it, thinking) Greek for a generation or more thereafter: some descendants of converts of the area still speak Greek. So the process of integration was a slow one.

The concomitant solution of apartheid, or separation, was the answer of the divorce court of A.D. 1453–54. Its definition was crucial. Given that race and religion could not be erased by Habit, that they had been engrained by the passage of Time, should the definition of separation be that of the rediscovery of their Greekness as a race by the intellectuals of the last generations of the Byzantine *Hochkultur*, like Manuel II or his prime minister Kydones (who was Greek as well as Latin)? Or was it to be the definition of the past, by religion: that Greeks were 'Roman' and Orthodox? It turned out to be the definition of the past. The Conquering Sultan's chosen patriarch, Gennadios II Scholarios (1454–56, 1462–63, 1464–65), was a member of an older anti-Latin intelligentsia.[21] So the Greeks in the end entered their Turkish house not as incipient Hellenes but as 'Romans'. The old slogan of 'Better the turban of the Turk than the tiara of the Pope', first voiced by patriarch Michael of Anchialos in the twelfth century, triumphed almost until 1821. In 1798 patriarch Anthimos of Jerusalem explained that:

> When the last emperors of Constantinople began to subject the Oriental Church to papal thraldom, the particular favour of heaven raised up the Ottoman empire to protect the Greeks against heresy, to be a barrier against the political power of the Western nations, and to be a champion of the Orthodox Church.[22]

For some Greeks at least, that heroic courtship, brief marriage with, and long separation from, the Turk became 'a kind of solution'.

NOTES

    *   The wording of this chapter differs little from the paper delivered at the University of Warwick on 30 November 1978, which explains why some of the demoticisms in it are more appropriate to a public lecture than a printed article. References have been kept largely to original sources quoted, beyond which the general reader may reasonably expect that such a large subject has attracted a synthesis readily available in English. This is true for the earlier period, where Speros Vryonis, Jr., *The Decline of Medieval Hellenism in Asia Minor and the Process of Islamization from the Eleventh through the Fifteenth Century* (University of California, 1971) is a fundamental analysis. But despite such useful recent surveys as Steven Runciman, *The Great Church in Captivity* (Cambridge, 1968);

D. A. Zakythinos, *The Making of Modern Greece From Byzantium to Independence* (Oxford, 1976); and A. E. Vacalopoulos, *Origins of the Greek Nation* (New Brunswick, 1970), there is no satisfactory account of the *Tourkokratia*, particularly from the Ottoman side – where H. Inalcik, *The Ottoman Empire: The Classical Age 1300–1600* (London, 1973) is the most recent survey. The Birmingham–Harvard project in late Byzantine and early Ottoman Demography (1978–82) is yielding evidence of how Ottoman conquest, conversion and assimilation worked and of the process of how some Greeks became Turks in two specific areas. But there remains a growing demand for a larger synthesis of the whole subject, towards which this paper can offer only a partial approach.

1. John Kantakouzenos, *Historiarum Libri IV*, vol. ii (ed.) L. Schopen, (Bonn, 1831) pp. 586–8; *cf.* A. Bryer, 'Greek historians on the Turks: the case of the first Byzantine–Ottoman marriage' (forthcoming).
2. S. Runciman, 'Teucri and Turci', in *Festschrift* for Professor A. S. Atiya (Utah, n.d.) 344–8; G. Parthey (ed.) *Hieroclis Synecdemus et Notitiae Graecae Episcopatuum* (Berlin, 1866; reprinted Amsterdam, 1967) pp. 20, 62, 105, 156, 168, 183, 204, 246.
3. Benjamin of Tudela, *Sefer Masa'ot (Itinerary)*, trans. A. Asher (London, 1907) vol. i, p. 310, vol. ii, pp. 172–5; A. Sharf, *Byzantine Jewry from Justinian to the Fourth Crusade* (London, 1971). Benjamin adds that they were friends with the Jews and that (like all pastoralists who have no fixed ovens or fields) they 'eat no bread and drink no wine, but devour the meat raw and quite unprepared'. He calls them '*Kofar Turakh*', '*kafir*', '*gavur*' or 'infidel' Turks – the same root as 'Gabras'. I am grateful to Dr Martin Goodman for transliterating the Hebrew.
4. E. L. Cutts, *Christians under the Crescent in Asia* (London, n.d.) pp. 46–7: 'It is said that the proclamation made at midnight from this minaret, and made with the hand before the mouth so as to disguise the words, is not the usual proclamation of the muezzins, but is a proclamation of the Name of the Holy Trinity. . . . The office of muezzin has been handed down from father to son in the same family; and to this day [1876] the listener can hear the voice from the minaret of Zecharah begin 'Kadoos Allah, kadoos, &c.' [i.e. the *trisagion*] and go off into an unintelligible cry. . . .' For other such examples, *see* F. W. Hasluck, *Christianity and Islam under the Sultans* (London, 1929).
5. S. Vryonis, Jr., 'Evidence on human sactifice among the early Ottoman Turks', *Journal of Asian History*, v (1971) 140–6; George Pachymeres, *De Michaele et Andronico Palaeologis* vol. i (ed.) I. Bekker (Bonn, 1835) p. 134.
6. S. Vryonis, Jr., 'The Greeks under Turkish rule', in N. P. Diamandouros and others (ed.) *Hellenism and the First Greek War of Liberation (1820–1830): Continuity and Change* (Thessaloniki, 1976) pp. 51–2; and the same's 'Nomadization and Islamization in Asia Minor', *Dumbarton Oaks Papers*, vol. xxix (1975) 41–71.
7. Discussed in A. Bryer, *The Empire of Trebizond and the Pontos*

(London, 1980) Study VII; *see also* C. Foss, 'Late Antique and Byzantine Ankara', *Dumbarton Oaks Papers*, vol. XXXI (1977) 42.

8. Nicetas Choniates (Acominatus), *Chronicle* (ed.) I. Bekker (Bonn, 1835) p. 50; *cf.* John Kinnamos, *Deeds of John and Manuel Comnenus*, trans. C. M. Brand (New York, 1975) p. 25.

9. C. Loparev, 'On the Unionism of the Emperor Manuel Komnenos', *Vizantijskij Vremennik* (1917) 344–57; *cf.* S. Runciman, *The Eastern Schism* (Oxford, 1955) p. 122.

10. I. Mélikoff, *La Geste de Melik Danişmend* (Paris, 1960); *cf.* Bryer, *The Empire of Trebizond*, Study VI.

11. Bryer, *The Empire of Trebizond*, Study IIIA.

12. S. Vryonis, Jr., *Decline* (London, 1971) pp. 473–5; P. D. Whitting, *Byzantine Coins* (London, 1973) pp. 262, 274; C. Cahen, *Pre-Ottoman Turkey* (London, 1968) pp. 264, 391, 398, 402; D. Talbot Rice (ed.) *The Church of Haghia Sophia at Trebizond* (Edinburgh, 1968) pp. 46, 55–82; Bryer, *The Empire of Trebizond*, Study V, 124. The miniature is in Topkapi Saray, Hazinedar Album 2153, f. 48b.

13. Bryer, *The Empire of Trebizond*, Study V, 119. The latest significant addition to the growing literature on Dede Korkut is Kh. Koregly, *Oguzskiy geroicheskiy epos* (Moscow, 1976).

14. Doukas, *Istoria Turco-Byzantina 1341–1462*, (ed.) V. Grecu (Bucarest, 1958) p. 59; trans. H. J. Magoulias, *Decline and Fall of Byzantium to the Ottoman Turks by Doukas* (Detroit, 1975) p. 73.

15. Choniates, *Chronicle*.

16. P. Charanis, 'Internal strife in Byzantium during the fourteenth century', *Byzantion*, vol. XV (1941) 230; J. Meyendorff, *A Study of Gregory Palamas* (London, 1964) pp. 195–7.

17. *The Letters of Manuel II Palaeologus* (ed. and trans.) G. T. Dennis (Washington, D.C., 1977); Manuel II Paléologue, *Entretiens avec un Musulman* (ed.) T. Khoury (Paris, 1966); *cf.* J. D. G. Waardenburg, 'The two lights, perceived: Medieval Islam and Christianity', *Nederlands Theologisch Tijdschrift*, vol. XXXI (1978) 276.

18. A. D. Alderson, *The Structure of the Ottoman Dynasty* (Oxford, 1956); C. Issawi, *An Arab Philosophy of History* (London, 1958).

19. *Cf.* S. Vryonis, Jr., 'The Byzantine legacy and Ottoman forms', *Dumbarton Oaks Papers*, vol. XXIII–XXIV (1969–70) 251–308.

20. Figures from H. W. Lowry, 'The Ottoman Tahrir Defers as a source for urban demographic history: the case study of Trabzon (*c.* 1486–1583)' (Los Angeles, 1977; unpublished Ph.D. dissertation).

21. Significantly, one of the earliest concerns of the first Ottoman patriarchs was the relaxation of Canon Law to preserve what could be done of Orthodox marriage and family structure. *See*, e.g., Ch. G. Patrinels, *Ho Theodoros Agallianos tautizomenos pros ton Theophanen medeias kai hoi anekdotoi Logoi tou* (Athens 1966) pp. 68–71.

22. R. Clogg, 'The "Dhidhaskalia Patriki" (1798): an Orthodox reaction to French revolutionary propaganda,' *Middle East Studies* (offprint) 87–115; *cf.* A. Bryer, 'The great idea', in A. Birley (ed.), *Universal Rome* (Edinburgh, 1967) pp. 100–17.

7 The Continuity of Hellenism in the Byzantine World: Appearance or Reality?

Robert Browning

In the world of today there are two cultures which appear to have maintained themselves without any sharp break in their tradition for more than 2500 years. They are Chinese culture and Greek culture. In both cases there is relative continuity of language, so that the earliest literature has remained accessible. Modern Mandarin differs considerably from Classical Chinese, and Modern Greek from Ancient Greek. But the differences between stages of Chinese and Greek are qualitatively distinct from those between Latin and French, or Anglo-Saxon and Modern English. In the one case we are faced with stages in the history of a single language, in the other with two distinct languages. Linguistic continuity, and the ensuing ease of access to literature of earlier epochs leads to continuity of values and ideals and terms of reference. During the Cultural Revolution in China one of the principal campaigns was directed against Confucius, who flourished about 500 B.C. Greek public men do not normally envisage the controversies in which they engage in such starkly archaising terms. But the appeal to examples of the past, and the readiness to make the past a model for the present, have always featured strongly in political oratory, journalism, and other modes of public communication.

Yet such an appearance of continuity may be illusory. I am not qualified to discuss the Chinese case. But in the Greek case many serious scholars have denied any significant continuity of culture between the ancient and medieval worlds, let alone the modern world. In the present paper I shall not deal with the growth of Greek nationality in modern times and the many problems which its study involves. I shall confine myself to the question whether the culture of the Byzantine world is in any meaningful sense a continuation of that of Ancient Greece, or whether the linguistic continuity conceals a radical break. Classical scholars, lured by the similarity of language to read Byzantine texts, have found themselves suddenly in a world whose style of life and values were bewilderingly different from what they had expected. And if they turned to the visual arts for reassurance of continuity, their bewilderment was all the greater. Some of them recoiled in a horror which verged upon disgust. Others sought to impose by force upon medieval writers the grammar of Attic Greek, an enterprise foredoomed to failure. Common to almost all of them was a certain loss of sense of direction, and a tendency to look on Byzantine culture either as decadent or as radically different from that of the ancient world.

Perhaps they were looking for something which could not possibly be there to find. For the antecedent of early Byzantine culture is not the Classical Greek culture of the city state, it is rather the long-lasting and intellectually rich culture of the Hellenistic age and the Roman empire. The Byzantine world was not the direct heir of the world of the Attic dramatists and Thucydides and Plato. Its immediate forerunner was the world of the Stoics, the Epicureans, the Cynics, and the Neoplatonists, of Plutarch, Lucian and Libanius, of Archimedes, Euclid, Ptolemy, Diophantus and Pappus — five mathematicians whose lives span more than five centuries —, of Theocritus and Callimachus and Nonnus, of Pseudo-Longinus, Demetrius and Hermogenes, of the Greek novelists, of Polybius, Posidonius and Cassius Dio, of Galen, of the origin and growth of Christianity. What we must try to establish is how far this culture was maintained and developed in the Byzantine world and how far it was lost, whether by deliberate rejection or by passive neglect.

It is revealing to survey the epigrams in which historians have summed up their view of the Byzantine world. For Edward Gibbon

it was 'the triumph of barbarism and religion'. For his older contemporary Voltaire, Byzantine history was 'a worthless collection
of orations and miracles', while for Montesquieu it was 'a tissue of
rebellious insurrections and treachery', and 'a tragic epilogue to
the glory of Rome'. These harsh judgements imply, among other
things, that little of Classical Greece survived in the Byzantine
Middle Ages. It is hardly surprising that the Greek historian Constantine Paparrhigopoulos (A.D. 1815—91) saw in the Byzantine
world 'a Greek renaissance', or that the Scottish philhellene
George Finlay, who devoted the greater part of a long life studying
the history of his adopted country, treated Byzantine history as 'a
portion of the history of the Greek nation'. For August Heisenberg
the Byzantine empire was 'the Christianised Roman empire of the
Greek nation'. Georgije Ostrogorski expressed the same view with
greater clarity when he wrote that 'Roman political concepts,
Greek culture, and the Christian faith were the main elements
which determined Byzantine development'. The French scholar
Charles Diehl was something of an odd man out in his view of
the Byzantine empire as 'an oriental monarchy'. His fellow-
countryman Paul Lemerle shows much greater insight when he
writes:

> From a pagan civilisation in the grip of decadence and
> incapable of self-renewal, Byzantium created a Christian one,
> more humane and responsive to the dictates of a critical con-
> science. And while assuring to ancient Hellenism this continuity
> of tradition . . . it added to it, both in art and in thought, the
> fruits of a long intercourse with the Persian and Muslim orient.

Finally, Karl Marx, speaking as it were off the cuff, called
Byzantium 'a golden bridge between East and West'. And N. H.
Baynes observed that 'an empire to endure a death agony of a
thousand years must possess considerable powers of recuperation'.

Insofar as these characterisations either expressly or by implication
deny the importance of Greek tradition in the Byzantine world,
they appear to base their denial on one or more of three arguments, all of which have been developed at length by various
scholars. These are:

1. That in spite of its Greek language the Byzantine state and
   Byzantine society were essentially a continuation of the Roman

empire, a political community of Italian origin and universalist claims, of which Greeks formed only an accidental element.

2. That in late Antiquity or the early Middle Ages Byzantine society was subjected to so much foreign penetration and influence that the reality beneath the Greek veneer had little to do with Greek tradition of life and thought. The Byzantine empire, according to this argument, resembled the Germanic kingdoms of western Europe, whose Latin culture concealed a fundamentally German society.

3. That the rapid Christianisation of the later Roman Empire, above all in the fourth century, marked a radical break in cultural continuity, and the birth of a society inspired by different aims and pursuing different values. This is the argument which underlies A. J. Toynbee's postulation of an Orthodox Christian Society distinct from ancient Greco-Roman society.[1]

Now there is some truth in all these formulations, which have provided rough and ready models for historians. The question is how much truth and what kind of truth. In the rest of this paper I shall examine critically each one of the three arguments which I have listed, in order to see whether it can be so revised and modified as to provide a better model.

First, the Romanity of Byzantine society. It is true that the Byzantine empire as a political entity is the direct continuation of the Roman empire, which embraced the whole Mediterranean world and much outside it. It was animated by a universalist and imperialist ideology, and was given new legitimation by Christianity. But in fact the vast eastern half of the empire, in which Greek was either the vernacular or the language of culture, was demographically, economically and culturally in advance of the Latin-speaking west. In the later Roman empire there was a curious division between the domains in which Latin and Greek were respectively used. The central administration, the army, and the law belonged to the Latin world, and an easterner who wished to participate in these activities had to learn Latin and often to adopt Latin culture. Obvious examples are the Antiochene Ammianus Marcellinus and the Alexandrian Claudian. Greek on the other hand was the language of city life, of trade, of science and learning. The roles of the two languages have recently been analysed with great penetration by Gilbert Dagron.[2]

The eastern, largely Greek, half of the empire withstood the on-slaughts of Germanic peoples more successfully than did the west. Much of the Latin-speaking world was lost to the empire in the fifth century, when Germanic kingdoms were established in Gaul, in Spain, in Africa, and in Italy itself. It is from this moment that two lines of policy can be discerned in Constantinople. One, the 'Roman', has as its aim the reconquest of the west and the restora-tion of a universal empire with strong Roman traditions. Its most obvious exponent is Justinian. The other policy, the 'Byzantine' rejects reconquest of the west as unattainable and irrelevant, and concentrates on the consolidation of the largely Greek east and the building up there of a power base capable of offering effective resistance to the Persians, and later to the Muslim Arabs. Anastasius and Heraclius both followed a 'Byzantine' policy. And in fact, after the Lombard invasion of Italy re-establishment of Roman power in the west was never a primary objective of any Byzantine government.

Even Justinian, champion of Romanity though he might be, issued most of his new legislation in Greek. And after his death Roman elements in Byzantine society rapidly lost what importance they once had. Heraclius abandoned the traditional Roman imperial titulature, with its resounding epithets going back to the days of Scipio Africanus, and began to call himself simply Βασιλεύς in official documents. The administrative reorganisation of the seventh century phased out the last vestiges of the old republican magistracies and of the traditional system of provinces. Of the Roman heritage there remained only Roman law – usually studied in Greek translations and adaptations,[3] a vague concept of the origin of imperial power in Senate, people and army which occasionally came to the fore when the succession had not been prearranged, a sense of mission and of inherent superiority to other societies and political communities, which was more often couched in Christian than in traditional Roman terms, and the name Ῥωμαῖος.

It is striking how infrequently Byzantine writers and speakers ever refer to Roman history before Constantine. They had avail-able the histories of Dionysius of Halicarnassus and of Cassius Dio – whether in the original or in the epitome by John Xiphilinus of Trebizond –, both of which could provide endless edifying or cautionary examples. The explanation must lie in a feeling that the pre-Christian Roman world was alien and irrelevant.

The Latin west in the Middle Ages certainly was alien. Tension between the Greek east and the Latin west grew through a series of misunderstandings and conflicts. Milestones in this path are the assumption of the imperial title by Charlemagne in 800, the Photian schism in the late ninth century, the final break between the eastern and western churches in 1054, the traumatic experience of the Crusades, the economic consequences of the trading and fiscal privileges which Byzantine governments found themselves forced to grant to western merchants, the paranoically anti-Latin feeling in Constantinople in the 1180s, and finally the disaster of the Fourth Crusade.[4]

During the long period of increasing estrangement between the Greek east and the Latin west — which growing acquaintance with one another only exacerbated — a transformation took place in the attitude of Latins and Greeks to one another. Each side developed a stereotype of the other which often had little to do with reality, but which served to focus their mutual distrust and contempt.[5] The Latins from being Romans — a character which they shared with the Greeks — had become 'Franks', with all the pejorative connotations of the term.

The re-establishment of cultural contact between east and west in the later Middle Ages was not easy. It was difficult for the Byzantines in particular, as it was closely linked with the question of church union. And the events of the previous centuries had made church union totally unacceptable to most Byzantines. Yet efforts were made to bridge the gap. Maximos Planudes realised that Latin literature had aesthetic merit and that its contents complemented that of Greek literature. So he translated some of Ovid and Juvenal, Cicero's *Somnium Scipionis* together with Macrobius' commentary, Augustine's *De trinitate*, Boethius' *Consolatio philosophiae*, and other works. Two generations later Demetrios Kydones saw that the theology of the Latins was fit to stand comparison with that of the Greeks, and translated Thomas Aquinas' *Summa contra gentiles* and much of the *Summa theologica*.[6] The rest of the latter work was translated by his brother Prochoros. Demetrios took the radical step of joining the Roman church. But Prochoros, in spite of his admiration for Thomist theology, remained Orthodox. By the end of the fourteenth century the westerners were beginning to realise how much they could learn from the Greek east. Niccolo de Niccoli, Chancellor of Florence, invited Manuel Chrysoloras to teach Greek in Florence. Chrysoloras brought with him not only Greek books, but a sophisticated tradition of study and a whole structure of aesthetic and moral principles.[7] His distinguished pupils − who included many of the leading humanists of the early Quattrocento − learned not only to read Greek, but what to read, how to read it, how to evaluate what they read. Incidentally they also learned from Chrysoloras how to write Greek, and modelled their hands upon his. A new study of Chrysoloras' role in the early Italian Renaissance is much needed.

By the later fifteenth century Italy was full of refugee scholars from the Byzantine east, each bringing his own contribution to the common pool of knowledge. A typical figure is the Athenian Demetrios Chalkokondyles, who taught Greek in Rome, Perugia, Padua, Florence and Milan, who numbered among his pupils men from beyond the Alps, such as the German Reuchlin and the Englishman Grocyn, and who prepared the first printed editions of Homer (1488) and Isocrates (1493).[8] Let us not forget his cousin Laonikos Chalkokondyles, who recorded with almost Polybian sweep and insight the growth of Ottoman power to fill the political vacuum created by the decline of the Byzantine empire.

The theme of the 'barbarisation' of Byzantine society is developed in two ways. The first argument is that foreign, and in particular oriental, elements played a predominant role in late antique and Byzantine society and that consequently what remained of Hellenic cultural heritage was swamped by foreign influences and reduced to the status of an insignificant vestige. The argument is not without foundation. It is certainly true that late Roman and early Byzantine society was polyethnic and multicultural − if one may make use of modern terms which do not quite fit ancient conditions. Apart from the Latin speakers in southern Italy, Africa, and the Balkans,[9] there was the large and influential Syriac-speaking population of Syria and Palestine, who formed part of a common Syriac ethnic community spreading across the Fertile Crescent from the gates of Antioch to those of Ctesiphon, there were the Copts of Egypt, the Armenians in the highlands of eastern Asia Minor, and many other less important ethnic and linguistic minorities. It was thanks to a Christian church whose leadership was firmly Greek that many of these minority groups developed a literature and a self-conscious culture of their own.

But the dominant culture was always Greek, and its attraction

drew in men from the minorities, who found that if they wished to
have more than local influence they had to use the Greek language
and work within the framework of Greek culture. There has been
no systematic study of the Hellenization of the intellectual élite of
minority groups during this period, though the question is one of
importance. A few examples must suffice. Romanos the Melode,
the greatest religious poet of the sixth century, who, if he did not
invent the *Kontakion*, certainly developed it into an art form of
great richness and flexibility, was a Syrian from Emesa, probably
of Jewish origin, and familiar with Syriac liturgical poetry.
Damascius, the last head of the Athenian Academy, was a native of
Damascus. His migration to Persia after the closure of the
Academy by Justinian was no doubt made the more easy by his
familiarity with the common culture of the Fertile Crescent in
which both Rome and Persia shared. There are also striking
examples of non-Hellenisation. St Daniel the Stylite stood on his
pillar near Constantinople from A.D. 460 to 493, and was visited
and consulted by many of the great men of the empire, including
the emperors Leo and Zeno. He never troubled to learn Greek, and
his utterances had to be translated from his native Syriac by his
followers. But Daniel was evidently in every way an odd man out.
The future Pope, St Gregory the Great, spent many years as Papal
apocrisiarius in Constantinople, but is alleged to have known no
Greek. There certainly was a large and influential Latin-speaking
community in Constantinople in the later sixth century, with
which Gregory doubtless maintained close contact. But the
question of his knowledge of Greek seems to need re-examination.
John of Ephesus, though he lived for many years in Constantinople
and for much of the time was a protégé of Justinian in the Great
Palace, yet chose to write his *Ecclesiastical History* and his *Lives of
the Eastern Saints* in Syriac, albeit a very Hellenising Syriac, which
often looks like a literal translation from Greek. The relations
between the dominant Greek culture and the minority cultures
were clearly complex. It may be that had not religious divisions
alienated some of the largest non-Greek communities in the
empire, and the Persian and Arab conquests finally separated
them for ever from the Byzantine state and Byzantine society,
Byzantium might have developed into a genuinely multi-national
and multi-cultural society, in which different cultures and different languages enjoyed parity of esteem. But in fact the
dominant role of Greek culture was strengthened by the conquests

of the seventh century. Countless Armenians,[10] Syrians, Slavs and others played a prominent part and rose to high office — sometimes to the highest of all — in the Byzantine world. But they did so only by adopting Greek language and culture and Orthodox faith. No doubt they often retained strong links with their original culture and brought elements of it into the amalgam of Byzantine civilisation. But they never even conceived of challenging the dominant position of Hellenic culture.

The other form of the barbarisation argument is that put forward in 1830 by Johann Philipp Fallmerayer,[11] according to whom the Slav invasions and settlements of the late sixth and seventh centuries resulted in the expulsion or extirpation of the original population of peninsula Greece. Consequently the medieval and modern Greeks, argues Fallmerayer, are not the descendants of the Greeks of antiquity, and their Hellenism is artificial. The controversy which Fallmerayer's book began has generated more heat than light, and those who contributed to it have often, whether they realised it or not, been motivated by considerations of modern nationalism. In its extreme form Fallmerayer's thesis is now generally abandoned, although R. J. H. Jenkins recently tried to give it new currency.[12] It is based upon an uncritical use of a few texts torn from their context and sometimes of very doubtful status anyway. And it reflects the Romantic vision of the world which the Bavarian Fallmerayer shared with many of his contemporaries.

The argument is invalid for several reasons.

1. Because the central areas of the Byzantine empire, in which the majority of the Greek-speaking population lived, Constantinople and Asia Minor, were not invaded or settled by Slavs. The population remained solidly Greek as far as the foothills of Armenia.

2. Because the original population was not extirpated or expelled from peninsula Greece. Many coastal regions and cities remained in Byzantine hands. Many mountainous and inaccessible areas became refuges for the indigenous inhabitants who had been uprooted from their homes. There was from the beginning a complex symbiosis between the newcomers and the remaining indigenous population, which will be discussed later. And it has recently been pointed out that during the Dark Age the Greek element in the Peloponnese was actually strengthened by immigration from Sicily and elsewhere.[13]

3. Because, as Isocrates long ago observed, being a Hellene was not a matter of genetics or tribal membership, but of culture.[14] He who speaks Greek and lives in Greek style is Greek. This continued to be the case in the Byzantine world; the only additional requirement was the profession of Orthodox Christianity. Many leading Byzantine families were believed to be of foreign origin, but were not discriminated against in any way because of this.

Let us not, however, throw the baby out with the bathwater. Fallmerayer was right in drawing attention to the extensive Slav invasion and settlement in continental Greece, which is strikingly borne out by the distribution of place-names of Slavonic origin.[15] What he and his adherents failed to emphasise sufficiently was the rapid and successful acculturation of the numerous 'Sklaviniae' in Greece.[16] This was a complex process, involving a number of factors. First of all there were economic relations. From their earliest arrival the Slav peasants, settled in small villages, must have exchanged their surplus produce for the industrial products of the surviving Greek cities, even if at first such trade was confined to a few essential tools, such as axes, and perhaps commodities of everyday use, such as textiles. No Slav settlement in Greece has been excavated, so we cannot trace in detail the beginnings of the economic relations between Slavonic countryside and Greek city which are later well attested, particularly in Thessalonica. Then there were political and military relations. Slavonic tribes sometimes aligned themselves temporarily or permanently on the Byzantine side and served as mercenary soldiers. Slav prisoners of war were resettled in various parts of the empire. We occasionally glimpse this aspect of Greco-Slav relations; as, for instance, when the brothers-in-law of the empress Irene, exiled to Athens, escape and take refuge with a Slav prince in Thessaly, in just the same way as nearly a century earlier Justinian II, exiled to Cherson fled to the protection of the Khagan of the Khazars, and later sought and obtained the support of the Bulgar ruler Tervel. Furthermore the emergent Slav ruling class – which owed its origins in part to the economic and political relations which we have described – was attracted by Greek life and Greek ways. The *Miracles of St Demetrius* preserve the story of Perbundos, chief of a Macedonian Slav tribe, who lived in Thessalonica, wore Byzantine dress, spoke fluent Greek, and was arrested on suspicion of preparing an attack against Thessalonica. A deputation of citizens of Thessalonica and Slavs went to Constantinople to intercede on his behalf.[17] Lastly, the church carried out missionary activity among the Slav settlers in Greece. These were the principal factors which led to the Hellenisation of most of the Slavs of peninsula Greece by the end of the ninth century.

The situation in Greece contrasts sharply with that in the northern Balkans. There were probably fewer Greek speakers remaining there after the Slav migration. But above all the existence of the Bulgarian state provided an alternative centre of power, and made Byzantine life less prestigious. After the conversion of Bulgaria in 865, and especially after the adoption of Tsar Symeon of the Slavonic liturgy for the Bulgarian church, it became possible to become a Christian, and hence to enter the civilised world, without adopting Greek culture or Byzantine allegiance.

The Christianisation of late Roman society certainly marked a radical change in values and life-patterns. But the Christianity of the fourth century had long left its Palestinian Jewish origins behind it. Christianity had become firmly rooted in the urban society of the eastern provinces of the Roman empire, which was largely Greek in language and culture. Even in the Latin west the early Christian communities were often Greek. The church of Lugdunum in the later second century was Greek-speaking. The church of Rome continued to use Greek as its liturgical language until the late third century, and perhaps even later. There are still Greek vestiges preserved in the liturgy of papal inthronisation.

But a condition and a result of the spread of Christianity among the urban upper classes was its reconciliation, so far as this was possible, with Hellenistic philosophical thought. The new faith had to become intellectually respectable in order to be accepted by the élite of late antique society, and this in spite of the protestations of radical groups who believed, with Tertullian, that Athens had nothing to do with Jerusalem. Clement of Alexandria, who died about A.D. 215, was perhaps the first to attempt a systematic 'philosophical' interpretation of Christian doctrine. His successor in Alexandria, Origen (185–253/4), was less preoccupied with explaining Christianity to the pagan upper classes. But in his polemical writings addressed to his fellow Christians he often assumes familiarity with the concepts and methods of Greek philosophy. In the later fourth century Gregory of Nyssa gave what amounted to a Neoplatonist interpretation of Christian theology. In the early sixth century Leontius of Byzantium applied Aristotelian logic to problems of Christology with the utmost finesse, while his contemporary Pseudo-Dionysius the Areopagite in the only original dogmatic work produced by the Orthodox church provided a thoroughly Neoplatonist version of Christian theology, which is almost a mirror-image of the pagan theology of Proclus.[18] At the same time, in Alexandria, John Philoponus commented on Aristotle's *Physics* and *De anima* and on the basic problems of Christian theology with the same sovereign command of Hellenic philosophical tradition and the same creative insight. All these thinkers sought to interpret Christianity in philosophical terms, not from suspect motives or from intellectual woolliness, but because they were convinced that only the best would do for the service of God. For them and their contemporaries the best meant not only the language and style of the Second Sophistic but also the syncretistic, Platonising world-view which was predominant in late Antiquity.

So the Christianity which permeated every activity of the Byzantine world had already been Hellenised, and grafted on to a great tradition of thought which went back to Plato, if not to Thales and Heraclitus. This was not something which concerned only intellectuals. The whole tone of Byzantine Christianity was optimistic, elastic, occasionally Panglossian, and very different from the more sombre, guilt-ridden Augustinianism of the Latin west. There was always room for οἰκονομία, for recognition of the distinction between the ideal and the actual.

The Byzantines were well aware of the two sources of their culture, Hellenic and Christian. They regularly called them τὰ θύραθεν ('what is from the outside') and τὰ ἡμέτερα ('what is ours'). But for most Byzantine thinkers and writers these were not alternatives, between a choice which must be made. They were rather constituent parts of a common heritage. This consciousness of two pasts emerges at a superficial level in the Byzantine habit of quoting Homer and the Bible side by side to make a point. It is manifest at a much deeper level when men like Michael Psellos or Theodore Metochites or Nicephorus Gregoras express their conviction that the two parts of their culture are compatible if they are understood correctly, and refuse to reject any of the Classical Greek intellectual tradition. A noteworthy example is Psellos' letter to the patriarch John Xiphilinus, who had accused him of being a Platonist rather than a Christian. Ἐμὸς ὁ Πλάτων, he begins, and goes on to declare that syllogistic reasoning is neither contrary to dogma nor the private preserve of philosophers, but a means of discovering truth.[19]

Extremists sometimes sought to reject one or the other of the two halves of the Byzantine cultural tradition themselves and to force their choice on others. The balance was a delicate one, which could easily be upset by excess of zeal. Monastic circles often practised or affected total rejections of τὰ θύραθεν. The Hesychasts of the fourteenth century and later frequently condemned those who pursued the study of Greek literature beyond an elementary level. On the other hand we have the pupil of John Italos who threw himself from a promontory into the sea, crying 'Receive me, Poseidon'. And in the last days of the Byzantine world George Gemistos Plethon ended up by turning his back on the whole Christian–Hellenic synthesis, though he did so only in his esoteric writings addressed to a coterie of Platonising pupils.

Within the mainstream of Byzantine thinking there were different currents, of which now one and now another prevailed. One broad distinction is that between what for want of better names we may call 'Aristotelian' and 'Platonic' attitudes towards classical literature. The 'Aristotelian' looks on classical literature primarily as material for training in logical thought or as a source of factual information. He is interested mainly in the work of historians, philosophers, orators and writers on technical and scientific topics, and is ill at ease with Hellenic poetry, which he rightly perceives to be concerned in large part with the irrational part of the mind, the emotions. And the emotions are the province of the church. It is some such consideration which explains the choice of reading of Photios and the books which Arethas had copied. The 'Platonists' on the other hand were interested in poetry and had a sense of the mysteriousness of things. Their explorations of the pagan background of classical literature laid them open to charges of heresy, atheism, and black magic.[20] Perhaps the curious inaugural lecture of Michael of Anchialos, the future patriarch as Professor of Philosophy (ὕπατος τῶν φιλοσόφων) in the 1260s, in which he undertakes to stick to Aristotle and to keep well clear of Plato, is another indication of this long-standing conflict.

Yet poetry was read and studied, and never left the school curriculum. And the devout John Mauropous begged God to save

from damnation Plato and Plutarch.[21] The Neoplatonist tradition
was studied not only in its Christian guise, but in the works of its
pagan masters. In spite of occasional official discouragement
Proclus was highly esteemed in the middle Byzantine period.
Michael Psellos was steeped in his works. The Georgian John
Petritsi, perhaps a pupil of Psellos, translated and commented on
Proclus' *Elements of Theology* at the beginning of the twelfth
century.[22] Excerpts from Proclus, including some from works now
lost, were made by a certain Isaac Sebastocrator or Isaac Porphyrogenitus, who must be either Alexios I's elder brother or,
more probably, the son of John II.[23] Later in the twelfth century
Nicholas of Methone wrote a long and philosophically interesting
refutation of Proclus' *Elements of Theology*, in which he alleged
that many of his own contemporaries had been led astray by
Proclus. There is much evidence, direct and indirect, of the copy-
ing of manuscripts of Neoplatonist philosophers in the middle
Byzantine period.[24]

The growing confrontation between the Byzantine east and the
Latin west made the Byzantines more conscious of their links with
Greek Antiquity, and of the privileged position in which their possession of the Greek language placed them.[25] Hellenic tradition
and Orthodox religion became the marks of national identity,
which distinguished the Byzantines not only from Jews, Muslims,
and pagans, but from their fellow Christians both in the west and
in the Slavonic world. Ἕλλην from its New Testament sense of
'pagan', which it had retained throughout the earlier Byzantine
period, came to mean 'Greek', 'Byzantine'. Nicephorus Blem-
mydes in the thirteenth century speaks of the Nicaean empire as τὰ
τῶν Ἑλλήνων σκῆπτρα. And already before 1204 panegyrists had
praised the Empress Euphrosyne, consort of the corrupt and selfish
Alexios III, for her Hellenic descent. This sense of ethnic and
cultural identity, with its twin marks of Hellenism and Orthodoxy,
was inherited by the late Byzantine world of the Palaeologan
period.

Thus far we have spoken of the attitudes of intellectuals and men
of letters, who leave written monuments behind them. There are
plenty of indications of popular attachment to elements and
aspects of Greek tradition, existing side by side with simple
Orthodox piety. Naturally such indications are scattered and dis-
connected and do not permit the kind of analysis which has been

attempted in the earlier sections of this paper. For what they are
worth, here are a few.

1. Alexander the Great remained something of a folk hero. There
   are numerous popular Byzantine and immediately post-Byzan-
   tine versions of the Alexander-Romance of Pseudo-Callis-
   thenes.[26] There is even evidence of a Christian Alexander.
2. When Digenis Akritas built a great palace in the mountains
   east of Cappadocia, which must have represented the average
   Byzantine's ideal dwelling, he had it decorated with mosaics.
   The subjects of these included, side by side with Biblical
   scenes, representations of Achilles, Agamemnon, Bellerophon,
   Odysseus, and Alexander.[27]
3. The popularity of Achilles is attested not only by the existence
   of a vernacular Achilleid in two versions — which has nothing
   to do with the Tale of Troy — but by the extraordinary story of
   a church in the Troad in the thirteenth century, in the narthex
   of which there was depicted a young man in military dress and
   labelled 'The Prophet Achilles'.[28]
4. There is a striking lack of Biblical material in early vernacular
   Greek literature. Joshua would make a splendid hero, and a
   cycle of pictures depicting his exploits is preserved in the Joshua
   Roll. Yet there is no Joshua poem. It is not until after the
   capture of Constantinople by the Turks that part of the Old
   Testament was paraphrased in demotic verse by George Chumnos.[29] It would appear that in the Byzantine period men sought
   heroes to admire or to identify themselves with in the classical
   part of their heritage.

The change from even the most 'decadent' Classical art of late
Antiquity to the art of the Byzantine Middle Ages is certainly striking. Yet we can no longer speak of a sharp dichotomy between
naturalistic, illusionistic, classical art and 'abstract' Byzantine art,
whose roots are to be sought in the ancient orient. The oriental
contribution to Byzantine art is real enough. But the investigations
of Weitzmann, Kitzinger, Demus, Talbot Rice, Lazarev and
others have drawn attention to the strong classicising and naturalistic element in much Byzantine art. I have neither the space, nor
the competence, to treat the subject in any detail, and will confine
myself to a few remarks of general application.

The first is that in the visual arts, as in literature and thought, τὰ θύραθεν and τὰ ἡμέτερα live side by side, and on the whole peace-ably. The superb David plates from Cyprus, with their combination of Biblical theme and classical iconography and style are exactly contemporary with the stiff and schematic, flatly abstract, mosaics of St Demetrius in Thessalonica. Among the sixth century icons of Mount Sinai one finds a very dematerialised, symbolic Virgin and Child and an amazing, almost impressionist, John the Baptist. Even within the same work − and in work by a good artist, both 'classical' and 'abstract' features may coexist. In the floor mosaics of the Great Palace in Constantinople − generally dated to the age of Justinian, but the question is still open − which are on the whole classical and illusionistic, one finds wholly schematic trees in no definable spatial relationship to the figures in the composition.

Just as in literature and thought, now one tendency prevails, now the other. So we can speak of classicising 'Renaissances' in the tenth century, in the twelfth century, in the fourteenth century, and so on. This question has been explored with great ingenuity and perceptiveness by Kurt Weitzmann.

A more important point is that 'abstract', symbolical art, though its historical origins may be in the passionate, religious world of the Fertile Crescent, has also Greek intellectual roots. The problem of 'representing the unrepresentable' is one familiar to Greek thought. Plato was much occupied with the relation of form to object and of object to its pictorial or other representation. And much of his negative attitude to art arose from his conviction that works of art − which evidently moved him deeply − were at several removes from reality, mere shadows of shadows. Plotinus made the very important observation that a work of art may not merely imitate what is visible, but may represent directly those intellectual entities of which the visible world is an emanation or derivation.[30] It was this Neoplatonist sense that an artist can rise above his particular model that underlay many of the traditional Byzantine attitudes towards sacred images in the worship of the church. In their way the Iconodules had a firm grasp of the Greek intellectual tradition.

Finally, Byzantine art, however 'abstract' and symbolic it may become, does not become merely decorative, as does much Islamic art. The artist is always concerned with the human figure. This persistent anthropomorphism fits Byzantine art to be the vehicle of the Christian doctrine of salvation through the adoption by God of human form. It is equally compatible with the Neoplatonist conception of the deification of man. The artist, even an 'abstract' artist, who is essentially concerned with man is forced to turn again and again for inspiration and models to classical, naturalistic, representations of man. And so the attempt to rise above the particular and the accidental can sometimes lead artists and their patrons back to classicism rather than away from it.

These are some of the ways in which the Byzantines came to terms with their challenging heritage of Hellenism. They were often conscious of the dead weight of millennary tradition. Theodore Metochites speaks of the difficulty of living as successors to the great men of the past, and of the feeling that everything worth saying had been said, everything worth doing done. Yet on the whole they were not daunted by being the heirs of Hellenism. They neither denied their heritage, nor reproduced it mechanically and timelessly. They absorbed it by using it to provide an intellectual basis for their moral and spiritual life, and in the end making it the cornerstone of their own communal identity, no longer just as Romans, or as Christians, but as Greeks, a term which over the centuries has acquired ever new overtones without losing its primary connotation.

NOTES

1. A. J. Toynbee, *A Study of History*, vol. I (London, 1934) pp. 63–7 and *passim*.
2. G. Dagron, 'Aux origines de la civilisation byzantine: Langue de culture et langue d'état', *Revue Historique*, vol. CCXLI (1969) 23–56.
3. P. E. Pieler, 'Nirgendwo anders als in der Einstellung zum Recht ist die Kontinuität zwischen Rom und Byzanz inniger' in H. Hunger, *Die hochsprachliche profane Literatur der Byzantiner*, vol. II (Munich, 1978) p. 343.
4. S. Runciman, *The Eastern Schism* (Oxford, 1955).
5. On western attitudes towards the Byzantines *see* B. Ebels-Hoving, *Byzantium in westerse ogen 1096–1204* (Assen, 1971).
6. K. Setton, 'The Byzantine Background to the Italian Renaissance' *Proceedings of the American Philosophical Society*, vol. C (1956) 52–7.
7. Ibid., pp. 57–8; R. R. Bolgar, *The Classical Heritage and its Beneficiaries* (Cambridge, 1954), pp. 268–71; J. Thomson, 'Manuel Chrysoloras and the Early Italian Renaissance' *Greek, Roman and Byzantine Studies*, vol. VII (1966) 63–87, where references will be found to earlier studies.
8. D. J. Geanakoplos, *Interaction of the "Sibling" Byzantine and Western Cultures in the Middle Ages and Italian Renaissance (330–1600)* (New Haven, 1976) pp. 231–64. In general on Greek influence on the Italian

Renaissance *cf.* the judicious survey by E. Garin, *La cultura del Rinascimento* (Bari, 1967) pp. 34–45.

9. On the Latin of the Balkans *cf.* the recent exhaustive survey by H. Mihaescu, *La Langue Latine dans le Sud-est de l'Europe* (Bucarest–Paris, 1978).

10. *Cf.* most recently A. P. Kazhdan, *Armyane v sostave gospodstvuqushchego klassa Vizantijskoj imperii v XI-XII vv.* (Erevan, 1975) esp. pp. 136–68.

11. J. P. Fallmerayer, *Geschichte der Halbinsel Morea während des Mittelalters*, vol. I (Stuttgart–Tübingen, 1830).

12. R. H. J. Jenkins, *Byzantium and Byzantinism* (Cincinatti, 1963).

13. Marilyn Dunn, 'Evangelism or Repentance. The Rechristianisation of the Peloponnese in the ninth and tenth centuries', in D. Baker (ed.), *Studies in Church History*, vol. XIV (1977) pp. 71–86.

14. Isocrates, *Panegyricus* 50. But *see* Polymnia Athanassiodi-Fowden, 'The Idea of Hellenism', Φιλοσοφία vol. VII (1977) 336 for a critique of the traditional interpretation of Isocrates.

15. *Cf.* M. Vasmer, *Die Slaven in Griechenland* (Berlin, 1941).

16. On acculturation of the Peloponnesian Slavs *see* A. Bon, *Le Péloponnèse byzantin* (Paris, 1951) pp. 64–76.

17. P. Lemerle, *Les plus anciens recueils des Miracles de Saint Démétrius*, vol. I, Le texte (Paris, 1979) pp. 208–9.

18. *Cf.* R. T. Wallis, *Neoplatonism* (London, 1972) pp. 161–2; B. Tatakis, *La philosophie byzantine* (Paris, 1949) pp. 24–5.

19. U. Criscuolo, *Michele Psello. Epistola a Giovanni Xifilino* (Naples, 1973). The passage here paraphrased occurs on p. 53.

20. M. A. Sangin 'Vizantijskie politicheskie deyateli pervoj poliviny X v', in *Vizantijskij Sbornik* (Moscow–Leningrad, 1945) pp. 228–49.

21. P. de Lagarde, *Iohannis Euchaitorum metropolitae quae in codice Vaticano graeco 676 supersunt* (Gottingen, 1881) No. 43.

22. E. R. Dodds, *Proclus, The Elements of Theology*, 2nd edn (Oxford, 1963) pp. xli–ii.

23. J. F. Kindstrand, *Isaac Porphyrogenitus. Praefatio in Homerum* (Uppsala, 1979) pp. 18–20.

24. M. Sicherl, 'Platonismus und Textüberlieferung', *Jahrbuch der Österreichischen Byzantinischen Gesellschaft*, vol. XV (1966) 201–29.

25. Hélène Ahrweiler, *L'ideologie politique de l'empire byzantin* (Paris, 1975) pp. 61–4.

26. G. Veloudis, *Der neugriechische Alexander. Tradition in Bewahrung und Wandel* (Munich, 1968).

27. Digenis Akritas, *Grottaferrata Version*, 7.59–101, (ed.) J. Mavrogordato (Oxford, 1956).

28. N. Festa, *Theodori Ducae Lascaris epistolae* (Florence, 1898) p. 310.

29. G. Chumnos Ἡ Κοσμογέννησις (ed.) G. A. Megas (Athens, 1975).

30. Plotinus, *Enneads*, 5.8.1. 32–40.

8 Archaeology in Greece

Paul Cartledge

Despite the well-known adage, the Greeks did not always have a word for it. 'Archaeology' has of course an ancient Greek etymology. But when the word was invented in the fifth century B.C., it did not mean what we would understand by archaeology but something like 'antiquarian lore'.[1] This is not to say that the ancient Greeks were not interested in matters archaeological. Far from it. For example, in about 470 B.C. the Athenian general Cimon, son of Miltiades of Marathon fame, dug up the alleged bones of the mythical hero Theseus on the island of Skyros and had them reburied in Athens – an early instance of politically motivated excavation.[2] And about seventy years later Thucydides, the great Athenian historian of the Peloponnesian War (431–04 B.C.), provides the earliest recorded 'excavation report' (1.8.1.): 'during the war the Athenians purified Delos, removing the tombs of all those buried on the island. Over half of these turned out to be Carians [non-Greeks], recognizable both by the range of weapons interred with them and by the manner of burial – still followed in Caria'.

Here then are the theory and practice of archaeology. Or are they? Obviously not, at least not as we would understand them today. For both Cimon and Thucydides had got their facts wildly wrong and, what is more, they lacked the technical and conceptual apparatus even to know how to go about getting them right.[3] We should not, however, be too hard on them. The rise of modern archaeology has been a painfully slow and fitful process, and scientific archaeology is barely a century old.[4] So in a lecture series entitled 'Greece Old and New' it seems appropriate to begin with a very rapid sketch of the development of archaeology in

Greek lands down to our own day. Thereafter I shall select the three most important archaeological sites of central and southern Greece – Delphi, Olympia and the Athenian akropolis – partly to illustrate the general development already described, and partly to introduce some of the more spectacular recent finds or familiar artefacts that can still be made to yield startlingly new information. Running through my commentary will be a theme whose identity will emerge in due course.

We begin, almost inevitably, with what has been unkindly called 'the Western world's biggest cultural cliché'[5] or, as the architectural correspondent of the *Observer* would have it, 'the most beautiful building in the world'.[6] The earliest surviving sketch of the Parthenon's west front, the elevation that confronts you as you emerge on to the summit of the akropolis through the Propylaia or monumental gateway, is by the peripatetic Cyriac of Ancona (Ciriaco de' Pizzicolli, see Plate 3b). Cyriac was an Italian merchant who spent the best part of thirty years in the first half of the *Quattrocento* travelling through Italy, Greece and the eastern Mediterranean. His drawings of Greek antiquities and his copies of Greek inscriptions provided the Renaissance with its only significant glimpse of *Greek* archaeology[7]; partly for geographical reasons and partly for political ones, the Renaissance's interest in the tangible remains of Classical Antiquity was mainly confined to what had been the western half of the Roman Empire.[8]

However, Cyriac was not exactly a slavishly faithful recorder of what he could see. The number of the Parthenon's columns is correctly given, but their profiles and proportions are haywire. Besides, although more of the pedimental sculpture was in place in the fifteenth century than today (for reasons given below), even that Cyriac preferred to represent in accordance with Italian Renaissance preconceptions. He did rather better in our eyes when he visited the sanctuary of the Great Gods on the island of Samothrace in the north Aegean. At least, his surviving drawings of the dancing women on a fourth-century B.C. frieze-block from the gateway of the sanctuary do convey the spirit of the original.[9] But then he unfortunately spoils this favourable impression by jumping to the conclusion that the figures represent seven of the nine Muses and labelling them arbitrarily in accordance with this fantasy. It is not accidental perhaps that Klio, Muse of History, is not included by Cyriac.

In 1453, five years after Cyriac had hung up his Hermes boots, the Ottoman Turks occupied Constantinople; in 1456 they took Athens, in 1458 the Peloponnese. Thereafter what we might call a muslin curtain descended, isolating Greece and the Aegean from the cultural developments of Western Europe.[10] In 1575 a Greek from Nauplia wrote of the ruinous state of Athenian antiquities that 'Today, only the skin remains; the animal that was in it has perished.'[11] It was not in fact before the seventeenth century that a fuller awareness of Greek antiquities percolated to the west; and we might single out the contribution of Thomas Howard, second Earl of Arundel, the first great English art-collector. Much of his collection of Greek (and Roman) sculpture and inscriptions, known as the Arundel marbles, eventually went to the University of Oxford and is now exhibited in the Ashmolean Museum.[12]

God, however, was not to be outdone by Mammon. Also in the seventeenth century the Capuchins and Jesuits established branches of their orders in Athens and naturally enough took a lively interest in the physical remains of the city where St Paul had 'stood up before the Court of Areopagus and said: "Men of Athens, I see that in everything that concerns religion you are uncommonly scrupulous"'.[13] However, the monks' archaeological knowledge fell rather short of their pious enthusiasm: the Parthenon, for example, was identified as the temple of the 'Unknown God' whose altar had been seen by St Paul. Still, the monks undoubtedly did anticipate one of the many invaluable functions performed by a modern Greek museum — that of conservation. For example, the fourth-century B.C. choregic monument of Lysikrates was built into the Capuchin monastery and used as the library of the Father Superior (see Plate 4a).

It is perhaps the latter who is represented contemplating mortality in the foreground of the drawing, but the illustration has another point of more immediate relevance. For it is a drawing by James Stuart, nicknamed Athenian Stuart, who with Nicholas Revett spent the years from 1751 to 1753 sketching and measuring what they later published as *The Antiquities of Athens*.[14] From the mid-eighteenth century onwards, under the influence of Winckelmann above all,[15] the remains of Classical Greece came to command as much attention as the Classical remains from further west. To begin with, however, it was hardly a disinterested academic attention. Museums and private collectors wanted *objets d'art*, while the aim of Stuart and Revett was to provide models for

Neoclassically-minded British architects.[16] That, incidentally, is why their drawings, unlike those of their predecessors, are architecturally accurate. Indeed, Stuart was himself commissioned to design replicas of several ancient monuments, for example of the famous first-century B.C. Tower of the Winds,[17] which he incorporated into a 1760s folly still standing at Shugborough in Staffordshire.[18]

The stay in Athens of Stuart and Revett was financed by the still extant Society of Dilettanti. In 1764 the Society took further advantage of the newly-awakened interest in Greece by sponsoring a complementary 'Ionic' expedition.[19] It was placed under the leadership of an Oxford don named Richard Chandler, who as an epigraphist had just published an edition of the Arundel Marbles. Moreover, it included Revett, by now estranged from Athenian Stuart.[20] Between 1764 and 1766 the expedition toured Greece and Asia Minor, and not least of its legacies are the fine watercolours — for example, of the Temple of Apollo at Didyma in southern Turkey[21] — painted by the expedition's official artist William Pars.

Pars was a good artist in his own way, but he was a dwarf in comparison to the Venetian Giambattista Piranesi. Those who visited the exhibition at the Hayward Gallery in 1978 celebrating the bicentenary of Piranesi's death will remember that at the very end of his life he produced a suite of etchings entitled 'different views of some remains of three great buildings which still stand in the middle of ancient Pesto' (Roman Paestum, Greek Poseidonia), in southern Italy. The 'great building' whose interior is illustrated here (see Plate 4b), is not in fact a Temple of Neptune (Poseidon) as the caption states, but one of the two Temples of Hera.[22]

By 1778, then, the 'Greek Revival' had penetrated the consciousness of the greatest Italian artists. It was now only a matter of time before the first international archaeological expedition to Greece was launched. This was duly undertaken in 1811 by a party of British, German and Danish architects and travellers including C. R. Cockerell, who later designed the present Ashmolean Museum in Oxford.[23] After pouring a libation in Athens to speed Lord Byron on his return to England, the party crossed over to the island of Aegina. Braving the perils of malaria and brigandage, they retrieved what they could from the fairly well-preserved Temple of Aphaia (at first wrongly identified as of Jupiter Panhellenius). An amusing drawing by Cockerell shows some members of the expedition perched intrepidly on the Temple itself, while others are studiously reading or making plans under canvas in the foreground.[24]

The impressive remains of the limestone Temple are now a major tourist attraction, but the equally impressive (and art-historically pivotal) pedimental sculptures are not, as the English participants had hoped, in the British Museum. Indeed, the Munich Glyptothek has just completed a costly programme of res-toring them to the state they were in when Ludwig of Bavaria bought them in 1812, and so removing the 'restorations' effected at Rome by the Danish Neoclassical sculptor Bertel Thorvaldsen.[25] Such are the caprices of artistic fashion.

Ten years after the 'excavations' at the Aphaia sanctuary the Greek War of Independence from the Turks was begun in 1821. In 1837, just six years after the successful conclusion of the war, the Archaeological Society was founded in Athens. Since then it has conducted many important excavations, notably on the Athenian akropolis, as we shall see.[26] The Society still flourishes, but yet more important is the work of the Archaeological Service, founded in embryo in 1835 and now a branch of the Ministry of Education. In addition to its routine activities the Service, through its thirty-seven Ephorates, may conduct up to eighty rescue excavations in a year as urban development and the building of roads and dams impinge on buried antiquities.[27] For what Cicero said of Athens in the first century B.C. is just as true of Greece as a whole in the twentieth century A.D.: 'wherever we step, we seem to be walking on a piece of history'.[28]

The Greek contribution to Greek archaeology since the 1830s has been enormous. But I may perhaps be forgiven for patting the odd *barbaros* (non-Greek) on the back too. And when I say 'odd', I mean just that, because archaeologists do not come much stranger than Heinrich Schliemann. We need not of course believe the romantic fable that Schliemann was fired with a passion to learn ancient Greek by hearing a drunken miller recite Homer. But it is certainly true that, after making a million in business by the age of forty-one, Schliemann spent the rest of his life doggedly trying to prove that Homer was a historian as well as an epic poet.[29]

In 1870 he began to investigate a mound in north-west Turkey which he thought was Homer's Troy. To be more precise, he drove a massive trench through the mound with the help of a railway engineer. Nonchalantly slicing through five superimposed cities, he hit upon one that to his businessman's eyes seemed rich enough to explain why the Greeks should have spent ten Homeric years besieging it. A famous photograph depicts Schliemann's Greek wife Sophia dripping with part of what her husband optimistically called 'The Treasure of Priam'.[30] In fact, though, as even Schliemann himself was later forced to concede, the treasure came from the city of a ruler about a millennium earlier than Homer's Priam — if, indeed, there was such a king.[31]

None the less, it was Schliemann's drive and enthusiasm in the field which revealed to the stay-at-home academics a whole subterranean world of Greek *pre*history undreamed of by them. Following his efforts in Turkey on the capital of Priam, Schliemann naturally turned his guns on the capital of Priam's adversary, Agamemnon. Excavations at Mycenae 'rich in gold' began in 1876, and the results were promptly published, with a dedication to his admirer Gladstone, two years later.[32] Of the finds the most spectacular was a grave circle containing six shaft graves, now labelled Circle A to distinguish it from its older contemporary Circle B excavated in the 1950s.[33] The graves in Circle A are now known to be at least three centuries earlier than any historical Trojan War. But Schliemann, when he came upon a remarkable gold death mask in shaft grave V (see Plate 6a), predictably telegraphed the Kaiser that he had 'gazed upon the face of Agamemnon'.

Still, for all his technical crudity and historical naïvety, Schliemann did have the archaeologist's nose for a good site. After his Herculean labours in Turkey and mainland Greece he wished to excavate the capital of the fabled pre-Homeric Cretan ruler, Minos, at Knossos. The Turks, however, who still controlled Crete, refused him permission — understandably perhaps in view of his cavalier attitude to the authorities when digging up Troy. More fortunate than Schliemann was a no less wealthy Englishman, Arthur Evans, who had first gone to Crete in 1894 to collect seals with engraved signs. Luckily for Evans, Crete was liberated in 1898, and the Greeks allowed him to buy the site of Knossos. Excavations began in 1899 and have continued in the Knossos area intermittently ever since. The wily Evans paid his local workmen on the wager system which he calculated would promote enthusiastic rivalry between the teams.[34]

Evans's methods, financial and otherwise, would not of course satisfy a modern archaeologist, let alone a modern Knossian workman. But at least by the time he started his dig at Knossos another Englishman, General Augustus Lane Fox Pitt-Rivers, had formulated the principles of archaeological stratigraphy and applied them on his ancestral estate at Cranborne Chase in Dorset.[35] The era of 'scientific' archaeology had dawned, and Evans was abreast of the latest developments. However, since Evans' death in 1941 a second scientific revolution has occurred in archaeology, and terms like radiocarbon dating and spectrographic analysis are as familiar to the archaeologist as they are to the physicist or chemist.[36] But there is still the need for less recondite skills like pot-mending, and it is one of the many legacies of Sir Arthur Evans that the chief conservator of the British School of Archaeology at Athens is a Cretan, Petros Petrakis.

Most of the pots mended by M. Petrakis come from normal excavations, such as the one at Myrtos in southern Crete directed by Professor Peter Warren of Bristol University.[37] But the menders who put together the bell-krater (wine-mixing bowl) depicted in Plate 6b were dealing with a pot with a more chequered history. Made at Athens in the 430s B.C.[38] it was exported − like so many of the best Athenian red-figure vases − to Etruria in Italy. Here it was unearthed in the eighteenth century A.D., rather than scientifically excavated, by what would nowadays be called 'tombaroli' (tomb-robbers). Eventually it was bought by Sir William Hamilton, complaisant husband of Lord Nelson's Emma and Plenipotentiary to the King of the Two Sicilies at Naples from 1764 to 1800, and became one of the thousand Greek vases in his second collection of Classical antiquities. (The first had already been sold to the British Museum.) To save the collection from the marauding French army in 1798, it was packed on to two British ships-of-the-line and despatched posthaste to England. One ship arrived safely. The other, HMS *Colossus*, sank off Samson in the Scillies, where it was rediscovered as recently as 1974. So far some 32,000 pottery fragments have been retrieved from the wreck in over 900 hours of underwater 'excavation'.[39] Here, then, we have a Greek excavation in British territorial waters conducted by methods that would have been unthinkable even twenty-five years ago.[40] This provides a fair measure of the yawning gulf that separates our archaeology from that practised in the fifteenth century by Cyriac of Ancona.

Thus far we have cursorily visited Athens, Samothrace, Didyma, Aegina, Troy, Mycenae, Knossos, Myrtos − and the Scillies. The remainder of this paper will be concentrated on Delphi, Olympia and the Athenian akropolis.

Cyriac in 1436 was the first Renaissance visitor to the site of ancient Delphi ('Wombs'). He grumbled, in Latin, that the benighted locals insisted on calling the place Kastri and knew nothing of Delphi's historic significance.[41] Two centuries later, a physician from Lyon wrote, to the same effect, that 'the most famous place in the world has suffered such a reversal of fortune that we were obliged to look for Delphi in Delphi itself, and to ask where the temple [of Apollo] was when we were standing on its foundations'.[42] It was not before the nineteenth century that interest in the site became at all lively.

In 1813 William Cam Hobhouse, to whom Byron dedicated *Childe Harold*, illustrated his account of *A Journey through Albania and other Provinces of Turkey in Europe and Asia* with a view of Delphi.[43] A quarter of a century later, exploration of the ruins was begun by a French architect, though this was not carried far: in 1849 Edward Lear (not all of whose output was nonsense) could still draw Delphi very much as it might have looked to Cyriac.[44] In 1892, however, all that was to change. Having secured permission to excavate from the Greek Government, the French School of Athens (founded in 1846) was granted an extraordinary credit from the French Parliament which enabled it literally to buy up and transplant the village of Kastri. The natives were understandably restless, but in 1892 excavations began regardless and have continued, with interruptions, to this day.[45]

As may be observed from contemporary photographs,[46] the French methods of excavation were at first not exactly irreproachable. Yet at least photography was available as an archaeological aid from the beginning of the excavations. In this century, however, photography has of course been developed and refined out of all recognition.[47] Thus we may now, for example, share with the Parnassus eagles a remarkable view of the sanctuary today (see Plate 5a).[48] At the top is the stadium (Roman in its present form) where the athletic events of the quadrennial Pythian Games were held. Below is the theatre, originally constructed in the third century B.C. Below that again are the remains of the fourth-century B.C. Temple of Apollo on whose foundations our disgruntled Lyonnais physician was standing in the late seventeenth century. The arrangement of the sanctuary as a whole may be more easily comprehended from the plan (see Figure 1).

I cannot of course take a long look at this plethora of buildings and their contents, so I shall concentrate for the moment on a

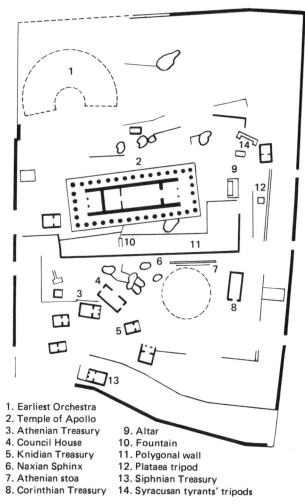

1. Earliest Orchestra
2. Temple of Apollo
3. Athenian Treasury
4. Council House
5. Knidian Treasury
6. Naxian Sphinx
7. Athenian stoa
8. Corinthian Treasury
9. Altar
10. Fountain
11. Polygonal wall
12. Plataea tripod
13. Siphnian Treasury
14. Syracusan tyrants' tripods

Fig. 1   Plan of Delphi

small building (marked 3 on the plan) that commanded an important turn in the Sacred Way leading up to the Temple of Apollo. The edifice in question is the so-called 'Treasury of the Athenians' built of marble from the island of Paros and restored to its present condition between 1903 and 1906 at the expense of the city of Athens (see Plate 5b). The date of its original construction is controversial. The general consensus of modern scholarly opinion apparently holds that it was erected around 500 B.C., but the

Baedeker of Antiquity, Pausanias (10.11.4) reported that it was set up to commemorate the celebrated Battle of Marathon, in which the Athenians, inspired by Miltiades, had defeated a vastly larger Persian invading force. Pausanias has his modern supporters, amongst whom I am inclined to number myself.[49]

When the discovery of the Treasury was announced in a telegram to Paris sent from nearby Amphissa, the zealous Prefect tried to intercept for the impoverished Greek exchequer what he imagined to be at least a small fortune.[50] Once, perhaps, the contents would have been worth a drachma or two, but there was, alas, nothing left by the beginning of this century. However, under the paving stones of the Sacred Way opposite the slightly later Athenian stoa (marked 7 on the plan) the French School made a remarkable — and unique — discovery in 1939.[51] I am justified, I think, in calling it a 'recent' find because the (restored) artefacts were only put on public display in the magnificent Delphi Museum in July 1978. The first published colour photographs of most of the major objects from this priceless find were printed in the 29 June 1978 issue of a popular Greek magazine rejoicing in the name of *Tachydromos*.

The objects I shall single out form part of a hoard of artefacts in ivory, gold, silver, bronze, iron and terracotta dumped together indiscriminately. They had clearly been damaged in a fire which had gutted a treasury like that of the Athenians, but had been reburied for reasons of piety. The fire probably occurred in the late fifth century B.C. (the latest datable object is the nozzle of an Attic terracotta lamp of *c.* 425 B.C.), but the most remarkable finds belong to the middle of the previous, sixth, century. These are the fragments of three statues in the chryselephantine or gold-and-ivory technique and a lifesize silver bull.

As we shall shortly see, the cult statue of Zeus at Olympia was also chryselephantine, but this and others mentioned in the literary sources are now lost, probably irretrievably. Hence the importance of the Delphi fragments, the only surviving specimens of this remarkable art-form yet discovered. In the Delphi Museum is displayed a reconstruction of the best preserved of the three figures, a seated Apollo. His wavy hair is made of gold, he wears a head-dress of long gold bands, and his face is of ivory with inlaid eyes. His full-length robe is embellished with plaques of sheet gold embossed with figures of animals both real and mythical. Apollo's arms have not survived, but his feet have; like the face, they are of ivory, and they are represented as shod with elaborately ornamental sandals.[52]

No less remarkable in its own way — and also unique — is a lifesize bull originally measuring perhaps 2.30 metres in length by 1.25 in height. It was fashioned in the *sphyrelaton* technique from hammered and shaped sheets of almost pure silver nailed over a wooden frame that has now perished utterly. The animal's horns, insides of the ears, forehead, nostrils, dewlap, hooves, genitals and probably the tip of the tail were all gold-plated. In the present state of preservation it is impossible to attribute a precise date and place of origin on stylistic grounds, but the excavator tentatively suggests that it was made by an Ionian master somewhere towards the mid sixth century B.C.[53]

Delphi, thanks to its oracle, became a panhellenic or all-Greek sanctuary in the mid eighth century B.C.[54] Perhaps rather earlier the sanctuary at Olympia of Apollo's father Zeus had acquired the same, panhellenic status. A scholar of the late fifth century B.C. calculated that the first Olympiad had been held in 776 B.C.,[55] and this date is even now officially taken to mark the inception of 'Greek History' in the most ancient English universities. But in the fifth century of our era the Christian Emperor Theodosius II finally banned the pagan Games, and in the sixth century nature added the finishing touches in the shape of a mighty earthquake followed by severe flooding. For the next twelve centuries a literally bucolic landscape, left Olympia's very location in doubt. In fact, the site was not correctly identified until 1765, by Richard Chandler. Ignorance, however, is bliss and offered generous scope for imaginative — and wisely anonymous — 'artistic reconstructions' of the sanctuary's appearance.[56] The archaeological reality was rather different.

In 1829 sober and realistic plans were drawn by the Expédition Scientifique de Morée which accompanied the French occupying force in the last stages of the War of Independence.[57] The Expédition also succeeded in partially clearing the great Temple of Zeus, but it was not the French who were destined to continue a project of excavation first mooted in the early eighteenth century by the distinguished French Benedictine scholar, Bernard de Montfaucon.

The kudos for that achievement went to the Germans, whose Archaeological Institute was established in Athens in 1874. The

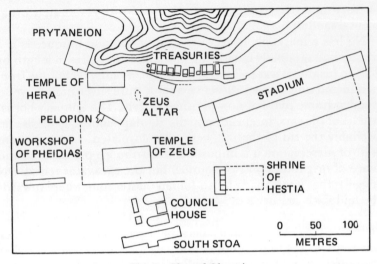

Fig. 2   Plan of Olympia

man most responsible for the realisation of the project was Ernst Curtius, and the contract drawn up between the Germans and the Greek Government set a precedent for future foreign excavations in Greece.[58] The Olympia campaign also inaugurated the era of scientific archaeology in Greece, although this would be hard to infer from photographs like that of the massed phalanx of picturesquely garbed workers carefully posed on the Temple of Zeus in 1875–6, the date of the first season.[59]

A century of excavation later, the plan of the sanctuary (Figure 2) has changed out of all recognition from that produced by the Expédition Scientifique de Morée. Among the most important results of the recent digging is the discovery that the stadium was originally sited considerably further west: what the many visitors now see is the fourth-century B.C., and later, site restored to something like its original appearance.[60] But far more spectacular than this solid gain in knowledge are the two recent finds that I have chosen to discuss.

You may perhaps recall the suggestion that the Treasury of the Athenians at Delphi was built to commemorate the Battle of Marathon in 490 B.C. With a remarkably well-preserved bronze helmet of oriental type rescued from a well by the north wall of the stadium we may approach even closer to the living reality of that historic victory (see Plate 6c). For running around the lower rim of the helmet is a *pointillé* inscription which tells us that the helmet was dedicated 'to Zeus by the Athenians having captured it from the Medes [Persians]'. It is not absolutely certain that it was after their victory at Marathon that the Athenians chose to include this magnificent artefact in a public dedication of spoils, but it is as near a certainty as such things can be. Stratigraphical considerations seem to favour a date early in the fifth century rather than towards the middle of it, the letter-forms of the inscription are consistent with a dating in the first half of the fifth century, and the famous victory virtually made it obligatory for the Athenians to dedicate a tithe of the spoils in the major sanctuary of the father of the Olympian gods.[61]

However, even this intriguing find pales by the side of my final exhibit from Olympia. The Temple of Zeus, you recall, was first uncovered in 1829 and naturally became the first objective of the German excavations of 1875. It was a splendid limestone structure, designed by a local architect and built between about 472 and 457 B.C.[62] The remarkably well-preserved figures from the pediments, recently moved to the new museum at Olympia, are the prime example of the so-called 'severe style' of Greek sculpture.[63] But it was neither the Temple itself nor the pedimental sculptures which chiefly aroused the awe and devotion of Antiquity. Those emotions welled up from contemplating inside the Temple the seated chryselephantine statue of Zeus, more than thirteen metres high, which ranked as one of the seven 'Wonders' of the ancient world.

When the Temple was excavated, no trace of the cult-statue was found — not unexpectedly, since it had been removed from Olympia by the Christian Emperor Theodosius I in the fourth century and perhaps consumed by fire at Constantinople in the fifth. However, there does survive an ancient description of the statue written by Pausanias (5.11) in the second century A.D. This makes it clear that not only the statue but also the throne was elaborately carved and ornamented with gold, ivory, ebony and precious stones. Furthermore, Pausanias gives directions to the site of the workshop where the statue was first assembled before it was again dismantled and re-assembled within the Temple itself. These directions lead to the site of a fifth-century Byzantine church just beyond the south-west boundary of the Altis or sacred precinct (Figure 2).

Careful excavations in and around the church in the 1950s

enabled the German archaeologists to confirm that this was the site of the workshop. Indeed, they were able to establish the workshop's method of construction and internal arrangement with sufficient confidence to build a scale model, which takes its place in the model of the sanctuary as a whole on display in the new Olympia Museum.[64] The workshop was divided internally by two spur walls, the statue being assembled in the deeper of the two chambers. Either side of the statue there was pillared scaffolding from which the craftsmen fitted the various bits and pieces on to the wooden core exactly as the designer prescribed. The designer's model from which they worked must have been a scale model no larger than one-fifth actual size.

The designer of the chryselephantine Zeus – to keep you in suspense no longer – was Pheidias, the Athenian who had overall artistic direction of the majestic remodelling of the Athenian akropolis undertaken after 448 B.C. (see below). Up until two decades ago the only evidence of Pheidias' physical presence at Olympia was the literary testimony of authors like Pausanias. Then between 1954 and 1958 the Germans made some exceptional discoveries to the south of the workshop. They found nothing less than the debris from the making of the statue.[65] This comprised chips of ivory and bone, pieces of obsidian (a volcanic glass), rock crystal, amber, gypsum, traces of red and blue dye, bone and bronze tools (including a goldsmith's hammer), clay matrices for hammering out the gold dress, and even moulds for making glass ornaments not mentioned by Pausanias. But the most plentiful category of finds was of course the virtually indestructible pottery, which had been used on site by the workers for eating and drinking and for ritual purposes.

Amongst the pottery fragments was a find almost too good to be true or, as the sceptical might have it, too true to be good. On the base of a small broken mug was scratched a neat graffito that reads: 'I belong to Pheidias'.[66] Nor is that all. The archaeological debris included some fine Athenian pots, which can be rather precisely dated, and none of them is earlier than about 435 B.C. In other words, either the Temple of Zeus, which had been completed by about 457, lacked a cult-statue for twenty years or more, or Pheidias' chryselephantine Zeus was not the first cult-statue. Moreover, in any event Pheidias' Zeus was designed and assembled after (not, as had been assumed by some, before) his chryselephantine Athena in the Parthenon, which was completed by 438.[67]

So his Athena set the standard he had to surpass at Olympia to produce a 'Wonder' of the ancient world.

Celebrated though his Olympian Zeus was in Antiquity, it is for his work on the Athenian akropolis that Pheidias is most widely known today. Pheidias was a personal friend of Pericles, the leading Athenian politician of the 440s and 430s, and it was Pericles who was mainly responsible for persuading the Athenians to undertake the monumental remodelling of the akropolis in about 450. It is a faint and blurred image of this remodelling that we see as we enjoy prospects of the akropolis today (see Plate 8a). The building pro-gramme was financed from the tribute raised ostensibly for a war against the Persian Empire, and it is to be wondered what the tributary allies of Athens felt about their money being used in this way.[68] Whatever they felt, it is worth being reminded that the Parthenon, on which I shall dwell for the rest of this paper, was a result and symbol of Athenian imperialism and that it was very likely constructed by the labour of non-Greek slave craftsmen as well as free Greek artisans.[69]

Cyriac of Ancona, with whose inaccurate sketch of the Parthe-non's west front I began, described the edifice appropriately as 'that vast and marvellous temple to the goddess Pallas'.[70] Although it had been converted into a Christian church and then a mosque, it was still pretty fine to look at when a series of rather more accurate sketches was made in 1674 (see Plate 7a). The artist was probably Jacques Carrey, a painter in the entourage of Louis XIV's ambassador to the Sublime Porte, who did altogether some fifty-five drawings of the Parthenon.[71]

It was, to say the least, providential that he did them when he did, for thirteen years later a 'prodigious bomb' (to quote the Venetian commander Morosini) turned the Parthenon into a shell-shocked ruin. The akropolis, which the Turks naturally used as their citadel and arsenal, was under siege from the Venetians in 1687, when a Swede fired a cannonball into the gunpowder stored in the Parthenon. It was not the least of the ironies that Königsmark, the Swede in question, had written a doctorate at a German university on the subject of 'The Misfortunes of Athens'. In a 1707 engraving (see Plate 7b) are depicted the trajectories of the fatal cannonballs, all converging on the Parthenon whose central portion is being blown sky-high above the minaret ominously — and artfully — placed at dead centre of the scene.

The Turks quickly recovered the akropolis, with continuing baleful consequences for the condition of the Classical antiquities thereon. Reluctant for security reasons to let any non-Turk on to the akropolis, the military governor had to be heavily bribed in the 1760s to allow William Pars to do the first close-up drawings of the Parthenon. What the governor most deeply objected to, it seems, was that Pars from his lofty vantage-point could overlook the women of the governor's harem who were kept in the Erechtheum!

In 1801 there occurred an event whose reverberations may still be felt around the world, from the Greek Parliament to the letters columns of the London *Observer*. I quote, *exempli gratia*, from a letter published in the *Observer* for 21 January 1979: 'I think it is high time that we of this country should return the Elgin Marbles to be restored to their rightful place, thus improving the condition of the ravished building. When I see the Elgin Marbles on the walls of the British Museum I can almost cry for their motherland'.

The author of this moving plea was Spike Milligan, and just as Edward Lear did not always produce nonsense, so Spike Milligan is not always comic. However, I do not propose to re-open here the investigation into 'Lord Elgin's crime'.[72] Suffice it to say that in 1801 Thomas Bruce, seventh Earl of Elgin and envoy extraordinary to the Ottoman court in Constantinople, obtained the Sultan's written permission to remove antiquities from the Athenian akropolis, whereupon he naturally removed as much of the Parthenon's figured sculpture as he could. Byron raged, both in *Childe Harold* and in *The Curse of Minerva*,[73] but the less romantic trustees of the British Museum shrewdly paid Elgin £35,000 for them in 1816, and they remain in the British Museum to this day.[74]

Half a century after Lord Elgin's appropriation of the Parthenon marbles the akropolis inspired the unknown painter of a watercolour now in the Benaki Museum in Athens. Nothing especially remarkable in that perhaps, but at roughly the same time — in May 1850, to be precise — a Frenchman stood on the akropolis, pointed his *appareil* at the interior of the Propylaia and produced a daguerrotype rightly included in the London *Sunday Times*'s 'Photodiscovery' series.[75]

Thirty-six years on, in 1886, another photographer captured an impressive scene of Greek workmen engaged in the Archaeological Society's important excavations on the akropolis.[76] It was these excavations which let out of the bag a cat Michelangelo for one would have been anxious to catch and skin alive. For the cache of marble statuary ceremonially reburied by the Athenians after the Persian sack of 480 B.C. revealed the awful truth that the Greeks had painted their pristine marble sculptures in garish blues, greens, reds and yellows.

Let us leave Michelangelo revolving in his grave and transport ourselves in imagination back to the year 432 B.C. Had we stood within the Propylaia then, facing east, the following scene would have presented itself (Figure 3). In front of us is the colossal bronze statue of armed Athena by Pheidias, so tall that the glint of her spear-tip was said to have been visible from ships off Cape Sunium. To the right (south-east) of the statue is the Parthenon, cunningly sited, like everything else on the akropolis, to make the most visually of its setting. To the left is a series of shrines and small ritual structures – no Erechtheum, since this was not built until the last decade of the fifth century.

This, then, was the view enjoyed by most Athenians at least once a year when they participated in the festival supposedly celebrating the birthday of their patron goddess Athena.[77] The birth itself was represented in the east pediment of the Parthenon. However, it is not the pediments of the Temple I want to consider finally, but the famous figured frieze (see Plates 6d and 8b). More than half of the frieze is now in the British Museum, but originally it ran all round the *cella* or central chamber (which housed the chryselephantine statue of Athena), measuring some 160 metres in length. Without question the subject of the frieze is a religious procession. The question is: what procession?

Professor Wycherley in his admirable recent book[78] is in no doubt whatsoever. It is the Panathenaic procession, that is to say the procession associated with the celebration of Athena's birthday mentioned above. This celebration was the greatest single event in the Athenian religious cycle, and every four years it was held with particular pomp and circumstance. A richly-patterned robe, woven by specially selected aristocratic Athenian girls, was then conducted in procession to the akropolis and draped around an ancient olive-wood image of Athena (not the chryselephantine statue).

Professor Wycherley's interpretation of the Parthenon frieze is what we might call the standard view. But even those who share this view are bound to admit that there are two giant obstacles in the way of its unconditional acceptance. First, if the interpretation is right, then the Parthenon would be the only known Greek

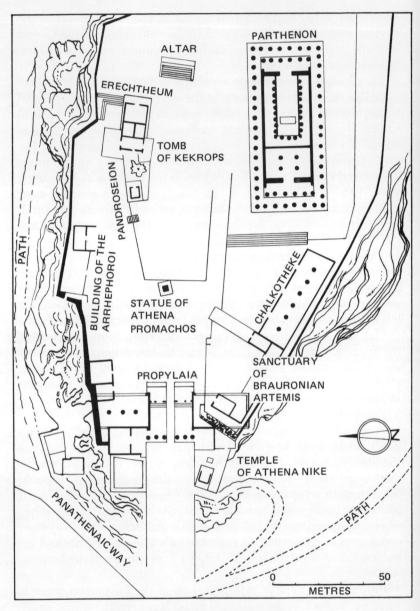

Fig. 3   Plan of Athenian Akropolis

temple whose sculptural decoration includes representations of living mortals involved in a real-life activity. Second, some elements which we know from literary sources to have been part of the actual Panathenaic procession are omitted from the frieze, while other elements which we would not expect to have been present or prominent are nevertheless represented there.

One way round these obstacles is that taken by Professor Robertson: 'the frieze is not a documentary record. It is . . . a highly sophisticated work of art, and as such highly selective'.[79] An opposite and equally justifiable reaction to the obstacles, which abandons the standard view, is to confess that they are not merely giant but cumulatively insurmountable. This is the line taken in 1977 by Professor Boardman in a paper of great originality.[80]

Professor Boardman begins by listing the known Panathenaic items missing from the frieze and the items present in the frieze that we would not expect to find in the actual Panathenaic procession. He then remarks on the inappropriateness of the Panathenaic procession as a subject to decorate the Parthenon, since the latter did not house the olive-wood image over which the new robe was draped every four years. Next, he points out that there is no parallel for the representation of deities, let alone the entire Olympian pantheon as here, as guests at a festival or sacrifice. Finally, he pertinently asks whether it is not odd that the gods should have their backs to the central scene being enacted on the east front, where the robe appears to be being handled.

Professor Boardman does not, however, wish to deny what he describes as the 'obviously Panathenaic character' of the whole frieze. Instead, he proposes to reconcile this overall character with the surprising omissions and additions by offering a novel inter-pretation. Now the main part of the procession on the frieze con-sists of horsemen and chariots. These are not, he suggests, living mortal horsemen but heroes – that is, semi-divine dead mortals who by their actions had acquired the right to depiction on public buildings and in the company of the immortal gods. At Athens in the third quarter of the fifth century B.C. there was just one such relevant group, the Athenian citizens who had died fighting at Marathon in 490 B.C. and were unquestionably worshipped as heroes after their death.

In the nature of things this hypothesis can never be finally proved, but Boardman is able to add a remarkable footnote – re-markable because, if it is right, it virtually clinches his arguments.

If one excludes from the calculation all those figures on the frieze who are unlikely or impossible candidates for heroisation, one is left apparently with 192 such figures.[81] This just happens to be the number of Athenians killed at Marathon as reported by Herodotus (6.117.1). Coincidence perhaps, but surely a divine — or at least a semi-divine — coincidence.

There, in conclusion, is an excellent example of how it is still possible to decant new wine from old bottles in Greek archaeology. It is also, as you have no doubt realised, the third and final illustration of my underlying theme — the Battle of Marathon, which, if John Stuart Mill is to be believed, was a more important event in *British* history than even the Battle of Hastings.[82] Fitting, therefore, that it should have been at Marathon that Byron's sailor 'dreamt that Greece might still be free'.

NOTES

* John Boardman and Michael Vickers kindly read a draft of this chapter and suggested many improvements. The remaining infelicities and errors are entirely my responsibility.

1. R. Pfeiffer, *History of Classical Scholarship, from the Beginnings to the End of the Hellenistic Age* (Oxford, 1968) pp. 51–4.

2. A. J. Podlecki, 'Cimon, Skyros and "Theseus"' bones', *Journal of Hellenic Studies*, vol. xci (1971) 141–3.

3. E. Pernice and W. H. Gross, 'Gelegentliche Bemerkungen zur Archäologie in der antiken Literatur', in U. Hausmann (ed.), *Allgemeine Grundlagen der Archäologie*, 2nd edn (Munich, 1969) pp. 448–65.

4. Glyn Daniel, *The Origins and Growth of Archaeology* (Harmondsworth, 1967); *A Short History of Archaeology* (London, 1981) and (ed.) *Towards a History of Archaeology*. (London, 1981).

5. Peter Green, *The Shadow of the Parthenon* (London, 1972) p. 12.

6. Stephen Gardiner, in the *Observer Colour Magazine*, 14 Jan. 1979, pp. 28ff.

7. Helen Hill Miller, *Greece through the Ages: as Seen by Travellers from Herodotus to Byron* (London, 1972) pp. 4–6; C. Mitchell, 'Ciriaco d'Ancona: fifteenth century drawings and descriptions of the Parthenon', in V. J. Bruno (ed.), *The Parthenon* (New York, 1974) pp. 111–23.

8. Roberto Weiss, *The Renaissance Discovery of Classical Antiquity* (Oxford, 1969); the discovery of the Greek world is discussed in ch.10.

9. E. W. Bodner and C. Mitchell (eds), *Cyriacus of Ancona's Journeys in the Propontis and the Northern Aegean, 1444–1445* (Philadelphia, 1976) p. 39 and n.75, figs 21–2. *See also* Phyllis Lehmann in P. W. and

K. Lehmann, *Samothracian Reflections: Aspects of the Revival of the Antique* Bollingen Series, vol. xcii (Princeton, 1973) pp. 3–56.

10. The East, as Mr St Clair puts it elsewhere in this volume, began at Belgrade.

11. Quoted in Miller, *Greece through the Ages*, p. 68.

12. D. E. L. Haynes, *The Arundel Marbles* (Oxford, 1975); *see also* the unpublished doctoral thesis of D. J. Howarth, 'Lord Arundel as a Patron and Collector 1604–1646' (Cambridge, 1978). A lavishly illustrated account of 'the lure of classical sculpture' between 1500 and 1900 is given in F. Haskell and N. Penny, *Taste and the Antique* (Yale, 1981).

13. Acts xvii.22 (New English Bible translation).

14. J. Stuart and N. Revett, *The Antiquities of Athens, Measured and Delineated*, 4 vols and supp. (London, 1762–1830). A colour reproduction of Revett's 'Stuart Sketching the Erechtheum' (1751) is printed in F.-M. Tsigakou's *The Rediscovery of Greece: Travellers and Painters of the Romantic Era* (London, 1981) pl. ii.

15. J. J. Winckelmann, *Geschichte der Kunst des Altertums* (Dresden, 1764); (repr. Weimar, 1964, ed. W. Senff).

16. J. Mordaunt Crook, *The Greek Revival* RIBA drawings series (London, 1968).

17. Stuart and Revett, *Antiquities of Athens*, vol. i, ch.3; plate 1 depicts the Tower of the Winds with the akropolis in the background.

18. Illustrated in R. Ling, *The Greek World* (Oxford, 1976) p. 28.

19. Joan Evans, *A History of the Society of Antiquaries* (Oxford, 1956) esp. p. 119.

20. R. Chandler, *Marmora Oxoniensia* (Oxford, 1763); and *Travels in Asia Minor and Greece: a New Edition with Corrections and Remarks by Nicholas Revett, Esq* (Oxford, 1825).

21. Reproduced in Ling, *Greek World*, p. 29.

22. John Wilton Ely, *Piranesi: Catalogue* (London, 1978) pp. 123–4. Piranesi, however, persisted in regarding the temples as Roman: N. Penny, *Piranesi* (London, 1978) p. 95. Note, too, that (*pace* Wilton Ely) only one of the three temples is of the fifth century B.C., the other two being of the sixth: W. D. E. Coulson, in *The Princeton Encyclopedia of Classical Sites* (Princeton, 1976) pp. 663–5.

23. C. R. Cockerell, *The Temples of Jupiter Panhellenius at Aegina and of Apollo Epicurius at Bassae near Phigaleia in Arcadia* (London, 1860); *cf.* D. Watkin, *The Life and Work of C. R. Cockerell* (London, 1974).

24. Reproduced in A. W. Johnston, *The Emergence of Greece* (Oxford, 1976) p. 27.

25. D. Ohly, *Die Aegineten: die Marmorskulpturen des Tempels der Aphaia auf Aegina; ein Katalog der Glyptothek München*, vol. i (Munich, 1976). On the Thorvaldsen Museum in Copenhagen *see briefly* G. Boesen, *Danish Museums* (Copenhagen, 1966) pp. 81–6; a learned exhibition catalogue is *Bertel Thorvaldsen: Skulpturen, Modelle, bozzetti, Handzeichnungen, Gemälde aus Thorvaldsens Sammlungen* (Köln, Wallraf–Richartz–Museum, 5 Feb. to 3 May 1977).

26. The results of the Society's excavations are published in its *Praktika* and *Ergon*.

27. A. Spawforth, formerly Assistant Director of the British School at Athens, kindly supplied this information.

28. Cicero, *De Finibus*, 5.1.5.

29. Leo Deuel, *Memoirs of Heinrich Schliemann* (London, 1978); *cf.* W. A. McDonald, *Progress into the Past: the Rediscovery of Mycenaean Civilisation* (Bloomington and London, 1967) ch.2.

30. Reproduced in P. M. Warren, *The Aegean Civilisations* (Oxford, 1975) p. 12.

31. H. Schliemann, *Troy and its Remains* (London, 1875); *Ilios: the City and Country of the Trojans* (London, 1880); *Troja: Results of the Latest Researches* (London, 1884). *See now* M. I. Finley, 'Schliemann's Troy — one hundred years after', *Proceedings of the British Academy*, vol. LXX (1974) 393–412 (also published separately).

32. H. Schliemann, *Mycenae: a Narrative of Researches* (London, 1878).

33. G. E. Mylonas, *The Grave Circle B at Mycenae* (Athens, 1972–3) (in Greek).

34. A. J. Evans, *The Palace of Minos*, 4 vols (London, 1921–36); *cf.* Joan Evans, *Time and Chance: the Story of Arthur Evans and His Forebears* (London, 1943) esp. pp. 308–51.

35. M. W. Thompson, *General Pitt-Rivers: Evolution and Archaeology in the Nineteenth Century* (Bradford-on-Avon, 1977).

36. *See* e.g. D. P. Brothwell and E. S. Higgs (eds), *Science in Archaeology* 2nd edn (London, 1969).

37. P. M. Warren, *Myrtos: an Early Bronze Age Settlement in Crete* (London, 1972); *cf.* Warren, *Aegean Civilizations*, pp. 61–6 (photograph of M. Petrakis on p. 65).

38. It is attributed to the Peleus Painter (a member of the 'Group of Polygnotos'), for whose *oeuvre* see J. D. Beazley, *Attic Red-figure Vasepainters*, vol. II 2nd edn (Oxford, 1963) pp. 1038–40, 1679; J. D. Beazley, *Paralipomena* 2nd edn (Oxford, 1971) p. 443.

39. Preliminary account by the director of excavations, A. Birchall, in *Illustrated London News* for Sept. 1978, pp. 71–5; for a semi-popular account by the discoverer of the wreck *see* R. Morris, *HMS Colossus: the Story of the Salvage of the Hamilton Treasures* (London, 1979).

40. *See* e.g. G. F. Bass, *Archaeology under Water* (London, 1966).

41. *cf.* G. Roux, *Greece* (London, 1958) p. 130: 'Deprived of its illustrious name, the "Navel of the World" became a hamlet of three hundred hearths, Kastri, where the sad grey houses had not even the whitewash that the villages of Attica and Cyclades throw over their poverty like the cloak of Noah.'

42. Jacob Spon (1678), quoted in Ling, *Greek World*, p. 24.

43. Reproduced in Miller, *Greece through the Ages*, p. 155.

44. Miller, *Greece through the Ages*, p. 159; or better in Tsigakou, *Rediscovery*, p. 111.

45. The results are published in *Bulletin de Correspondance Hellénique* and the series *Fouilles de Delphes*.

46. *See*, for examples, Johnston, *Emergence*, pp. 31, 67.

47. *See* generally E. Harp, Jr. (ed.), *Photography in Archaeological Research* (Albuquerque, 1975).

48. For some aerial photographs in colour of Greek sites *see* R. V. Schoder, *Ancient Greece from the Air* (London, 1974), esp. pp. 45–53 (Delphi). Satellite and shuttle photographs of Greece are now also available, though not yet easily accessible.

49. For a tentative post-Marathon dating *see* Johnston, *Emergence*, p. 70. However, J. Boardman, *Greek Sculpture: the Archaic Period* (London, 1978) fig. 213, gives a date of about 500–490 B.C.

50. Johnston, *Emergence*, p. 30.

51. P. Amandry, 'Rapport préliminaire sur les statues chryséléphantines de Delphes' *Bulletin de Corr. Hellénique*, vol. 63 (1939) 86–119.

52. The (unrestored) head and feet of 'Apollo' and the head of 'Artemis' are dated about 550–540 B.C. in Boardman, *Greek Sculpture*, fig. 127. The plaques referred to in the text have been published by Amandry, *Athenische Mitteilungen*, vol. LXXVII (1962) 35–71, Beil. 6–9.

53. Amandry, 'Statue de taureau en argent', in *Etudes Delphiques* (*BCH*, Supp. IV, Paris, 1977) pp. 273–93.

54. Cl. Rolley, *Fouilles de Delphes*, v. 3 (Paris, 1977), pp. 131–45.

55. Hippias of Elis, *Fragmente der griechischen Historiker* (ed.) F. Jacoby, 6F2.

56. An example is reproduced in Miller, *Greece through the Ages*, p. 293.

57. A. Blouet *et al.*, *Expédition Scientifique de Morée*, 3 vols (Paris, 1831–8).

58. For the history of exploration and excavation at Olympia *see* B. Fellmann, in B. Fellmann and H. Scheyhing (eds), *100 Jahre deutsche Ausgrabung in Olympia* (Munich, 1972) pp. 27–34.

59. Fellmann and Scheyhing, *100 Jahre*, fig. 29.

60. For the history of the stadium *see* briefly E. Kunze, in Fellmann and Scheyhing, *100 Jahre*, pp. 49–52.

61. Kunze, 'Ein Bronzhelm aus der Perserbeute', *Olympiabericht*, vol. 7 (1961) 129–37. The contemporary Greek helmet dedicated at Olympia by a Miltiades – Kunze, *Olympiabericht*, vol. 5 (1956) 69–74 – is not certainly the one worn by the brilliant Athenian general of that name at Marathon.

62. A. Mallwitz, *Olympia und seine Bauten* (Munich, 1972) pp. 211–34.

63. B. S. Ridgway, *The Severe Style in Greek Sculpture* (Princeton, 1970).

64. A. Mallwitz, 'Olympia im Modell', in Fellmann and Scheyhing, *100. Jahre*, pp. 61–70, esp. fig. 79.

65. A. Mallwitz and W. Schiering, *Die Werkstatt des Pheidias in Olympia* (Olympische Forschungen 5, Berlin, 1964).

66. Mallwitz and Schiering *Die Werkstatt*, pp. 151 (No. 9), 169 ff., pl. 64.

67. On the Parthenon Athena *see* R. Meiggs and D. M. Lewis (eds) *A Selection of Greek Historical Inscriptions to the End of the Fifth Century B.C.* (Oxford, 1969) no. 54.

68. We do hear of some internal Athenian opposition, but the evidence is far from impeccable: A. Andrewes, 'The opposition to Perikles', *Journal of Hellenic Studies*, vol. XCVIII (1978) 1–8, esp. p. 2.

69. For the employment of slave masons in the construction of the Erechtheum in the last decade of the fifth century *see* A. Burford, *Craftsmen in Greek and Roman Society* (London, 1972) p. 91.

70. Quoted in Miller, *Greece through the Ages*, p. 4.
71. The drawings may conveniently be studied in T. Bowie and D. Thimme (eds), *The Carrey Drawings of the Parthenon Sculptures* (Bloomington and London, 1971).
72. W. St Clair, *Lord Elgin and the Marbles* (Oxford, 1967); Carl Nylander, *The Deep Well: Archaeology and the Life of the Past* (Harmondsworth, 1971) pp. 145–54.
73. *Childe Harold's Pilgrimage*, ii, xi–xv. From *The Curse of Minerva* (composed 1811, published 1828) we might extract the following ringing apostrophe:
    Frown not on England; England owns him not:
    Athena, no! thy plunderer was a Scot.
74. E. Miller, *That Noble Cabinet: a History of the British Museum* (London, 1973) esp. pp. 102–7.
75. B. Bernard, '*The Sunday Times' Book of Photodiscovery* (London, 1980) pl. 17.
76. Reproduced in Johnston, *Emergence*, p. 29.
77. H. W. Parke, *Festivals of the Athenians* (London, 1977) pp. 33–50.
78. R. E. Wycherley, *The Stones of Athens* (Princeton, 1978) pp. 117, 206.
79. C. M. Robertson and A. Frantz, *The Parthenon Frieze* (London, 1975) p. 9.
80. J. Boardman, 'The Parthenon frieze – another view' in U. Höckmann and A. Krug (eds), *Festschrift für Frank Brommer* (Mainz, 1977) pp. 39–49.
81. 'Apparently', because the frieze is not wholly preserved; the calculation here followed is that of W.-H. Schuchhardt in *Jahrbuch des deutschen Archäologischen Instituts*, vol. xlv (1930) 274–8.
82. J. S. Mill, 'Grote's History of Greece' (1846), repr. in Mill, *Essays on Philosophy and the Classics*, collected works xi (Toronto, 1978) p. 273.

9   Byron and Greece

William St Clair

No major writer of modern times has been so closely involved with
the land of Greece as Lord Byron. Greek themes run through
nearly all his poetry, and they provided him with inspiration
whether he was being romantic or comic. 'If I am a poet', he told
Trelawny, 'the air of Greece made me one.'[1] Byron was influenced
by Greece, but he in his turn has influenced attitudes to Greece
and the Greek nation both in the West and in Greece itself. And
that I presume is why he is picked out for special treatment in this
series of lectures.

I shall discuss how Lord Byron and his poetry have affected per-
ceptions of Modern Greece. It is a hazardous and intractable
topic, for changes in attitudes and their causes are difficult to
measure; there is always a temptation to see connections where
they do not exist and to exaggerate the importance of particular
events; and with Byron the poetry is inseparable from the life and
the life from the myth.

The relationship between literature and political events was a
subject of much philosophic debate in the age of romanticism, and
as with so many questions, two opposing views are represented by
Byron and Shelley. For Shelley literature was all. In his essay *A
Defence of Poetry*, which was not published in his lifetime, he
argues that poetry is an unconscious power, a unique access to
knowledge, and a prophecy of things to come. Poets, he argues,
can bring about social and political change: poets are 'the unacknowledged legislators of the world'. Byron disagreed sharply.
He was always distrustful of such high falutin' claims. He seems to
have had a rather low opinion of the place of literature in the

scheme of things. All his life he longed to be a man of action, and it was only in the last year of his short life when he went to Greece that he began to feel that he was really making a contribution, the previous thirty-five years having been frittered away in frivolous activities such as poetry and love.

In retrospect we can see that Byron underestimated himself. His influence was immense and all-pervasive through much of the nineteenth century, although it often appears difficult to pin down exactly where it lies. It obviously did not derive solely from his poetry or from his ideas, which are for the most part neither particularly original nor particularly profound. Nor did it derive from his actions and accomplishments, for Byron, despite his longing to be a successful soldier and revolutionary, never achieved much in practice.

I am not going to offer a solution to the Byron puzzle here but I think Byron's impact on Greece, besides being of great interest in itself, throws light on the more general question of how the man, his works, and the myths they created have interacted on the wider world beyond literature.

I begin with Byron's first visit to Greece when he was a young man, for that set the course of his whole career. In 1809 Lord Byron was just turned twenty-one and was living the life of a typical Regency rake. He had inherited the title when he was three, and though not in fact rich, from the beginning, as schoolboy and student, he lived the life of extravagance, since he had virtually unlimited credit. He spent freely on clothes, women, gambling and much else besides. Newstead Abbey, his house near Nottingham, was the scene of many delightful and expensive orgies. In 1809 he and his friend Hobhouse were deep in trouble and had urgent reasons for leaving the country. They sailed from Falmouth in July, and Byron was away from England for almost two years.

Foreign travel was an established feature of the education of men of his class and a well-known device for escaping creditors and scandal. Had times been normal they would probably have gone on the Grand Tour — Paris, Switzerland and the Alps, carnival in Venice, Florence, and Easter in Rome. But it was wartime. Napoleon had closed most of the Continent to English visitors so they were obliged to go further afield — to the area which now consists of Albania, Greece, and Turkey. There were plans to go even further to Egypt and India, but in the event Byron spent most of his time in Greece.

Greece is today very much a distinctive country, but at the time of Byron's first visit it was a part of the huge sprawling Ottoman Empire, ruled by the Sultan in Constantinople, which still covered most of the Balkans and Middle East. The total population of the Empire was about thirteen millions, of which about a quarter were Greeks, and they were widely scattered in communities all over the Empire besides in the area now called Greece. The chief cities of the Greek world were Constantinople, Smyrna, and Bucarest; none of them, you will notice in the territory of present-day Greece, and few Greeks live in these cities nowadays. Athens was a mere village. The Piraeus was non-existent, except for a customs house and scattered ruins. Only in mainland Greece and in some islands were the Greeks in a majority, but everywhere there were large Turkish and Albanian minorities who had been settled there for hundreds of years and knew no other home.

They set the character of the place. If you look at pictures of a typical town in Greece at this time, the most distinctive features are the minarets of the mosques which dominate the skyline the way in which steeples do in the West. Greece was an Eastern country, for the East began at Belgrade, the frontier town between Christendom and the infidel world beyond.

The climate was very unhealthy. Malaria was endemic, and plagues swept the country nearly every year. To Europeans, Greece was probably almost as unhealthy as India or West Africa, and the life expectancy of the few merchants who settled there was short. Europe tried to keep itself free from the terrible oriental diseases by enforcing a quarantine − forty days in the lazaretto − and the line between East and West was a strict one.

Most travellers in Greece stuck to a set route which included the best known ancient sites. The 'Giro of the Morea' can still be recognised in some package tours. But most of the country was un-known. The standard guide-books which travellers took with them were still Pausanias, who wrote about A.D. 150, and Wheler, whose *Journey into Greece* was published in 1682 and was never reprinted. It was good fun to topographise, to visit villages with strange Venetian or Turkish names and try to identify them with the famous cities of Antiquity − Negropont − Chalcis; Salona − Amphissa; Castri − Delphi; Porto Leone − the Piraeus, and so on.

Byron belonged to the first generation of a type which was to become a familiar feature of the scene in Greece and elsewhere through much of the nineteenth century — the milordos or travelling gentleman. Greeks and Turks could understand how it might be necessary, from time to time, to go to the trouble, expense, discomfort and danger of travel for the sake of business or to make a pilgrimage. But to travel for *pleasure*, that was a peculiarly English madness and it still carried its own dangers. A contemporary writer gave this advice on travelling in Greece:

> Avoid having the air of examining Turkish fortresses. If you should be questioned about the motives of your tour, you may reply that it is the custom of your country and that you have read much of Greece in ancient books. . . . The most current notion is that you are in search of hidden treasure, it being impossible for them to conceive that you travel merely to examine the mouldering ruins of ancient towns and temples.[2]

The writer went on to warn against asking questions about agriculture or trade or figures of population, since the traveller might be suspected of spying.

Byron and Hobhouse travelled with two servants and two armed guards who often had to be reinforced. They usually had ten horses, six for riding and four for carrying the luggage. This luggage included three beds, two wooden bedsteads, a stove, cooking utensils, charcoal, cutlery, crockery, linen, in fact everything two English gentlemen might need for eighteen months of continuous picnicking. They had to carry a large quantity of money and gifts — guns, telescopes, snuff boxes. Chandeliers were often expected but I do not know if Byron's party carried any. As Hobhouse remarked, the delicacy of no soul in the Turkish Empire was hurt by a repayment of kindness in hard cash.

Dress was important. Travelling gentlemen were advised to carry three dozen clean shirts, since washing facilities were infrequent. They sometimes put on local dress — and you can see Byron's magnificent Albanian costume in the Museum of Costume at Bath, though I doubt if he wore it much except to have his portrait painted — but wearing Eastern dress could be risky, for, in some parts of the Ottoman Empire, Franks were known to have been summarily put to death for wearing a turban. Usually the travelling gentleman got himself fitted out with a colourful military uniform of his own design.

Travelling was expensive, intensely uncomfortable, and dirty.

Byron was also of the first generation to value personal cleanliness and clean linen (that owed much to Beau Brummell), and, as they were told proudly at Ioannina, the Albanian louse is the biggest in the world. However he accepted it all in the spirit of adventure, unlike his valet William Fletcher, whose attitudes were more typical of the English abroad. As Byron wrote when he had to send him home:

> Besides the perpetual lamentations after beef and beer, the stupid bigotted contempt for everything foreign, and insurmountable incapacity of acquiring even a few words of any language, rendered him an incumbrance. I do assure you the plague of speaking for him, the comforts he required, the pillaws which he could not eat, the wines which he could not drink, the beds where he could not sleep, and the long list of calamities such as . . . want of tea which assailed him . . . would have made a lasting source of laughter.[3]

I mention these mundane facts partly to emphasise how exotic and adventurous travel in Greece still was in Byron's day, but also because he himself liked to see his journey in these terms. He was not prepared to behave like a conventional tourist. Although he was very well grounded in ancient literature and ancient history, he took care to conceal it. Much of his time during a long stay in Athens was spent in riding, swimming, and sex, although I don't think we need take too seriously the figure of 200 which he used in one of his letters. When first shown the Parthenon he is supposed to have remarked that it was very like the Mansion House, and when Hobhouse or local guides tried to show him over some archaeological site he became bored and contrary. 'Antiquarian twaddle' he called it. I doubt if he would have wanted to attend this series of lectures.

For although few people had actually visited Greece, English literature was cluttered with conventions and clichés about Greece and about the Modern Greeks. Visitors to the country inevitably saw it in terms of their education, which was heavily slanted towards the classics, and when they wrote down their impressions their books helped to pre-set the opinions of their successors. It was very easy — and still is I guess — for visitors to Greece to be sentimental and patronising.

In Byron's day notions about the Modern Greeks were mainly concerned about their relationship with the Ancient Greeks. Are

Modern Greeks the blood descendants of Pericles and Miltiades? Frankly it is not a question that makes much sense. You can try to trace the numerous incursions of immigrants to Greece and attempt to assess the extent to which the 'Hellenic' blood of the ancients has become diluted by Romans, barbarians, Slavs, Franks, Turks, Venetians, Albanians and so on, but that approach carries assumptions about race and genetics which are simply wrong as well as being distasteful. Or you can look for evidence of cultural continuity, among which of course the amazing survival of the Greek language is the strongest. But neither approach takes you far if you are hoping for guidance on how to regard and treat the modern inhabitants of the country.

Most travellers in Byron's day simply assumed that the Modern Greeks were the descendants of the Ancient Greeks without bothering too much about the implications. They looked at their faces to see if they could find Grecian profiles familiar from ancient sculptures and vases. They wondered whether Modern Greek habits — love of arguing, love of the siesta — were survivals from ancient times. They liked to think of Modern Greeks as run-down or 'degenerate' Greeks, showing what happens to a great civilisation when it loses its sense of purpose. As representatives of a superior and successful civilisation, European travellers loved the image of degenerate Greeks living a simple life with their goats among the crumbling ruins of the great monuments of Antiquity.

A people who were so degenerate might aspire in time to be re-generated. In the years before Byron's visit, European ideas of liberty and nationalism, which received a tremendous boost by the French Revolution, had already reached Greece. The notion that the Greeks might throw out their Turkish rulers and take their place among the nations of Europe was already commonplace. It was a romantic dream long before Byron but nobody thought of it as practical or likely to happen.

While he was in Greece Byron was composing the first two cantos of a poem about his travels which he called *Childe Harold's Pilgrimage*. On his return he looked around for a publisher, and after some difficulty a minor bookseller called John Murray agreed to print an edition of 500 copies. It came out in March 1812.

It was on this occasion that Lord Byron woke up and found himself famous. The book sold thousands of copies and went through ten editions by 1815, a runaway best seller. It was translated into French and German and Italian and Byron's fame rapidly spread

all over Europe. After *Childe Harold* came a succession of other
poems, many with Greek themes – *The Giaour, The Corsair, The
Bride of Abydos, The Siege of Corinth* – all of which were
immensely popular. By the time he was thirty Byron was a European figure, as famous as the great Napoleon himself.

Childe Harold, upon which Byron's fame was based, is, among
much else, a political poem about the contemporary condition of
the Greeks. The Greeks are slaves, Byron proclaims. Only the
landscape and the climate are the same as in ancient times. It is no
good the Greeks looking to foreigners to help them, Byron shouts,
what Greece needs is violent revolution:

> In all save form alone how chang'd! and who
> That marks the fire still sparkling in each eye,
> Who but would deem their bosoms burn'd anew
> With thy unquenched beam, lost Liberty![4]

The Greeks will never be free until they imitate their ancient
ancestors:

> When riseth Lacedemon's hardihood,
> When Thebes Epaminondas rears again,
> When Athens' children are with arts endued,
> When Grecian mothers shall give birth to men,
> Then may'st thou be restored; but not till then.[5]

There is a contempt for the Modern Greeks for their ignorance and
failure of patriotism:

> Shrine of the mighty! can it be
> That this is all remains of thee?
> Approach, thou craven crouching slave,
> Say, is not this Thermopylae?
> These waters blue that round you lave,
> O servile offspring of the free –
> Pronounce what sea, what shore is this?
> The gulf, the rock of Salamis![6]

Note the evocative power of the ancient Greek names. No need to
remind a European audience of their associations. Note also the
implicit assumption that the Greeks are the descendants of the

Ancient Greeks, degenerate slaves passively accepting their humiliation among the memorials of their former greatness. (Incidentally the word 'lave' seems to exist in romantic poetry largely to provide a rhyme for 'slave' — we'll hear it again later.)

In the verse part of *Childe Harold* Byron's view is uncompromising but he was too intelligent a man to swallow his own propaganda. At the back of the book Byron printed numerous notes and appendices on points mentioned in the text. Some of this prose section of the book reads like extracts from a scrap book, and I am surprised that the publisher agreed to print it. Byron dismisses the notion that Greece might be independent, which he has advocated so passionately in the poem itself. 'The Greeks' he writes, 'will never be independent; they will never be sovereigns and as heretofore, and God forbid they ever should.'

Byron also acknowledges that it is nonsense to discuss the problems of Modern Greeks in terms of their putative ancestors — like discussing the future of Peru in terms of the Incas, he says. Anyway, he goes on, what does it matter if the Modern Greeks are descended from the Ancient Greeks? 'What Englishman cares if he be of Danish, Saxon, Norman or Trojan blood? or who except a Welchman is afflicted with a desire of being descended from Caractacus?'

Byron's ideas about Greece were not new or original. But never before had they been expressed with such power or their message been spread so widely all over the Western world.

Much of the appeal lay in the portrayal of the romantic hero — proud, passionate, melancholic, borne down by a load of guilt for some secret crime and cut off for ever from his fellow men, yet noble and generous and irresistible. Childe Harold was taken to be a thinly disguised picture of Byron himself, and though he denied it, it was true. For with Byron the appeal of the man was as powerful as the appeal of the poetry. From the moment of the publication of *Childe Harold* every detail about Lord Byron became intensely interesting and has remained so ever since.

The Greek setting of his poetic tales gave a suitable aura of romance and exoticism to readers who had never seen the Mediterranean.

Know ye the land where the cypress and myrtle
Are emblems of deeds that are done in their clime
Where the rage of the vulture, the love of the turtle
Now melt into sorrow, now madden to crime![7]

Byron shared in the glamour of Greece, but Greece in its turn was carried along by the glamour of Byron.

Innumerable paintings and engravings gave a visual reinforcement to the Byronic view of Greece: Classical ruins with goats in the foreground; monstrous Pashas sitting around doing nothing in particular except smoking long pipes and looking cruel and inscrutable; black-eyed girls, young, passionate, and uncomplicated.

In fact as a guide to the political situation of the Greeks, the notes to *Childe Harold*, which few people read, are much more reliable than the verse. It was by no means obvious to the Greek leaders of Byron's time that their future lay in establishing a European nation state by violent revolution. To use the idiom of modern economics and political theory there were other 'development models' in the field which were both more realistic and more attractive.

Capodistria, the most eminent Greek of today, put his faith in a gradualist approach, relying on a spread of education to liberalise the institutions of the Ottoman Empire. Others looked forward to the day when the Greeks − who seemed set to overtake the Turks as the dominant group in the Ottoman Empire − could take over the Empire itself, re-establishing a new Byzantium. The educated Greek classes (apart from the diaspora in Europe) lived mainly in Constantinople and were strong upholders of the Ottoman system, since they filled many of the best jobs in the Ottoman civil service, and they lorded it over some of the other peoples of the Empire, such as the Romanians and Bulgarians, as arrogantly as the Turks themselves.

Most Greeks did not share Byron's views and would not have understood his allusions. They did not think of themselves as Greeks at all − and certainly not as Hellenes (a word incidentally which always makes me uncomfortable) but as Christians or Orthodox. They had little sense of nationality in the Western European sense of a nation state like England or France with distinct geographical boundaries, a single language, and uniform culture. They thought of themselves rather as the Orthodox Christian inhabitants of a large multi-racial empire. They were not, for the most part, in the least interested in their ancient ancestors, and they knew very little about them. When travellers found the locals at Marathon or Salamis with stories about ancient times, they were delighted, for they thought they had found a genuine tradition from ancient times. But the locals were usually repeating stories they had heard from earlier travellers.

A friend of mine who was doing research into the life of Lawrence of Arabia was naturally thrilled to find a party of Bedouin living in tents in Jordan with an old man who spoke very confidently about Lawrence. It turned out later that he had derived his information from seeing Peter O'Toole and Omar Sharif in the film.

The orthodox church, the main unifying institution of the Greeks, was totally opposed to the spread of new-fangled western ideas. And when the custom started, again under western influence, of giving Greek children Classical names such as Pericles, Miltiades, Aristoteles and so on, the church authorities tried to suppress it, insisting that children should only be given saints' names or traditional Christian names, Constantine, Demetrios, Georgios, Hilarion.

The church fought long and hard against the growth of western ideas. In 1798 for example the Patriarch of Jerusalem issued a warning to his flock against the dangerous notion of Liberty.

> [The devil], he says, has devised in the present century another artifice and pre-eminent deception, namely the much vaunted system of Liberty which perhaps on the surface appears to be good so as to deceive if possible the chosen people. It is however a trap of the devil and a destructive poison, to drive the people headlong into corruption and confusion.[8]

Nowadays everybody is in favour of Liberty however much they differ in applying it in practice. The point is that in Byron's time Liberty was widely thought of in Greece as an alien western idea, rather as 'democracy' in the western sense is denounced by the religious leaders in present-day Iran. At the time of Byron's first visit in 1809–10 western nationalism had apparently made little progress in Greece itself. To take one example, while Byron was in Athens, the agents of Lord Elgin were still engaged in removing the sculptures of the Parthenon, a task which went on for several years. Byron included a bitter attack on Lord Elgin in *Childe Harold* which was taken up and followed by many other travellers. But the Greeks themselves do not appear to have minded much at the time or raised any protest at the destruction of their most powerful symbol of nationality. They simply did not think yet in those terms.

Within ten years of Byron's visit to Greece, everything had changed with the outbreak of the Greek Revolution in 1821.

The direct influence of Lord Byron and his poetry on the leaders and of the revolution was probably non-existent. But you notice at once from the voluminous pamphlet literature of the time that, right from the beginning, western Europeans could not see the events in Greece except in western philhellenic Byronic terms. The fighting was done by Greeks with their own aims and ambitions, but the political justifications were provided by foreigners or western educated Greeks. The history of the Greek Revolution — with its numerous internal conflicts and civil wars — reflected the struggle between the various development models open to the Greeks, but the western model which had a ready-made political vocabulary and a ready-made political mythology had a huge lead. Very soon the groups in Greece most bitterly opposed to the western notion of Greece were obliged to use the political language of their opponents and therefore to slip into their habits of thought.

Curiously, by the time the Greek Revolution broke out, Byron himself had abandoned the high romantic style of the Grecian tales that had made him famous. They were the views of his hot youth — now he was more aware of the complexities and contradictions of life and was attempting to catch them in *Don Juan*. The style is entirely different, mocking and colloquial instead of solemn and grandiloquent. But everywhere you look, there are evidences of his visit to Greece, often in the most unexpected places. Let me quote just one example — the three ladies that the Don met in the harem who are drawn from Byron's friends in Athens:

Lolah was dusk as India and as warm;
   Katinka was a Georgian white and red,
With great blue eyes, a lovely hand and arm,
   And feet so small they scarce seemed to tread,
But rather skim the earth: while Dudu's form
   Looked more adapted to be put to bed,
Being somewhat large and languishing and lazy,
   Yet of a beauty that would drive you crazy.[9]

But in 1821, the year of the Greek Revolution and of the publication of Canto III he reverted again to his philhellenic mood, breaking the texture of the poem, to include what is perhaps his most famous short poem, 'The Isles of Greece'. But this time it is not Byron who speaks, nor Childe Harold, nor any foreigner: the song is put into the mouth of a Greek sailor. The sentiments are the same. Again it is enough just to mention the ancient names to get the appropriate response. It is no longer a foreigner mourning the fate of Greece and despising its modern inhabitants, but a Greek conjuring up the spirit of his ancestors and a Greek making the ancient names vibrate with history and romance:

> The mountains look on Marathon,
> 　And Marathon looks on the sea;
> And musing there an hour alone,
> 　I dreamed that Greece might still be free,
> For standing on the Persian's grave
> 　I could not deem myself a slave[10]

At the same time his friend Shelley was at work on *Hellas* the last long poem he was to complete before his early death. Shelley was an intense admirer of Ancient Greece and he read its literature not as venerated masterpieces, but as living documents to illuminate his own life and times. In the preface to *Hellas* Shelley set out what is perhaps the classic statement of philhellenism, much of which he had derived from Byron:

> We are all Greeks − our laws, our literature, our religion, our arts, have their root in Greece. But for Greece, Rome would have spread no illumination with her arms and we might still have been savages and idolaters; or what is worse might have arrived at such a stagnant and miserable state of social institution as China and Japan possess. . . . The modern Greek is a descendant of those glorious beings whom the imagination almost refuses to figure to itself as belonging to our kind, and he inherits much of their sensibility, their rapidity of conception, their enthusiasm, and their courage.

Byron and Shelley spent the first six months of 1822 together at Pisa in Italy, in close contact incidentally with the expatriate Greek colony, until Shelley was tragically drowned in a storm at sea. Byron was desolated, he was tired of fame, and dissatisfied with his life. At the age of thirty-four his deep longing for the life of action pressed more urgently than ever. Although he had lived a life of unequalled intensity, he placed no great value on his poetry. He felt old and ill with even his power to love failing. Like so many of the great romantics he had a strong premonition that he would die young. It was then that he decided to devote himself personally to the Greek struggle and to go to Greece as a volunteer in the war.

As on his first visit, if you read his prose, you might think his attitude was cynical and even contemptuous towards the Greeks. 'Damned liars' was one of his favourite descriptions. He went to Greece, he wrote in his journal, in the spirit of Mrs Fry visiting Newgate Prison, not expecting to find any great examples of virtue there, but in the hope that the thieves and murderers might with care, in time, be reformed.

But this as usual was only one side of his character. In his poetry he showed another side. On 22 January 1824 at Missolonghi his secretary Count Gamba noted in his journal:

> This morning Lord Byron came from his bedroom into the apartment where Colonel Stanhope and some friends were assembled and said with a smile, 'You were complaining the other day that I never write any poetry now. This is my birth-day and I have just written something which, I think, is better than what I usually write'.[11]

His last great poem, like his first, was of Greece.

Tis time this heart should be unmoved
　　Since others it hath ceased to move
Yet though I cannot be beloved
　　Still let me love!

My days are in the yellow leaf
　　The flowers and fruits of love are gone
The worm, the canker and the grief
　　Are mine alone! . . .

If thou regretst thy youth, *why live?*
　　The land of honourable death
Is here. Up to the field and give
　　Away thy breath!

Seek out — less often sought than found
    A soldier's grave, for thee the best
Then look around and choose thy ground
    And take thy rest!

Byron died at Missolonghi not long afterwards of an illness
brought on by the unhealthy climate. It was not the soldier's death
he had wanted, in fact his contribution to the military side of the
war was insignificant. But Byron symbolised powerfully that the
nations of Europe were prepared to come to the aid of a small
people on the periphery of the continent. The name of Missolonghi
where he died was soon to be as resonant with associations as
Salamis and Marathon and the other ancient names he had
invoked so tellingly in his poetry. The funeral oration was delivered
by Spyridon Tricoupis who recognised at once the peculiarly
Byronic combination of literary imagination and political action:

> He has given his name to the age in which we live. The
> breadth of his intellect and the height of his imagination did
> not allow him to follow the splendid but well trodden path
> of literary glory. He took a new road . . . but as long as his
> writings live (and they will live as long as the world exists)
> this road will remain open since, like the other, it is a road
> of true glory.[12]

Tricoupis went on to become Prime Minister in independent
Greece and to write an influential history of the Greek Revolution
in which the notion of the Modern Greeks as modern Hellenes
fighting for Liberty was given a further impetus.

Within a year of Byron's death there also appeared, printed at
Missolonghi, a long poem in Greek by a young poet that Byron had
met briefly at Cephallonia. The 'Hymn to Liberty' by Solomos
became the Greek national anthem. It was written before Byron's
death, but it is highly Byronic in character.

One echo is amusing. You will remember the Byronic maidens
in 'The isles of Greece':

Fill high the bowl with Samian wine
    Our virgins dance beneath the shade
I see their glorious black eyes shine
    But gazing on each glowing maid
My own the burning tear-drop laves
    To think such breasts must suckle slaves

Solomos in his 'Hymn' picks up the reference. He too imagines the beautiful Greek girls dancing in the shade but he rejoices that their breasts are going to suckle Courage and Liberty.[13]

The Greek national anthem, with 158 verses, must be the longest in the world, and I do not expect there are many occasions to sing verse 83. But the Byronic influence is much more pervasive than just individual literary echoes, and generations of Modern Greeks have been unconsciously influenced by it.

By the time the Greek War of Independence came to an end and the independent Greek state was established, the Greeks themselves had already largely adopted the Byronic view of themselves which had previously been a rather ignorant fancy of foreigners. They saw themselves increasingly as descendants of the Ancient Greeks and increasingly as a modern European nation. During the nineteenth century this national myth − and I call it that without disrespect − advanced rapidly until the former rival alternative views of what the destiny of Greeks should be were largely submerged. One of the Governments, in the 1930s I believe it was, cut down the palm trees in Omonia Square, because palm trees were thought to give too Eastern a flavour to the capital city of Greece.

At the great crises, including the two world wars, Greece has consistently, sometimes after some wobbling, chosen to see herself as a Western nation. And the Western powers have consistently seen Greece in totally different terms from the other countries of the Eastern Mediterranean. I am not saying of course that this is all due to Byron, but at each crisis the memory of Lord Byron has contributed to the decision, and his ideas have influenced millions of people who know nothing of his life or work.

In Athens, on 28 May 1979, the Greek Government signed the Treaty of Rome, and in 1981 Greece became the tenth full member of the European Economic Community. Bureaucrats and Eurocrats now have to struggle with the resulting problems of the olive oil and wine lakes and the peach and citrus fruit mountains. Not many of them have read *Childe Harold's Pilgrimage* and I am not sure that I would recommend them to. But I would perhaps commend to them Shelley's *Essay on Poetry* with which I began. His final remarks contain, to my mind, a clear reference to Byron and are near to being the last word on the influence which Byron has exerted on Modern Greece:

It is impossible to read the compositions of the most celebrated writers of the present day without being startled with the electric life which burns within their words. They measure the circumference and sound the depths of human nature with a comprehensive and all-penetrating spirit and they are themselves perhaps the most sincerely astonished at its manifestations: for it is less their spirit than the spirit of the age. Poets are the hierophants of an unapprehended inspiration, the mirrors of the gigantic shadows which futurity casts upon the present; the words which express what they understand not; the trumpets which sing to battle and feel not what they inspire; the influence which is moved not but moves. Poets are the unacknowledged legislators of the world.

NOTES

1. Trelawny, *Records of Shelley, Byron and the Author* (Harmondsworth, 1973) p. 83.
2. Rev. Philip Hunt, quoted by W. St Clair, *Lord Elgin and the Marbles* (Oxford, 1967) p. 67.
3. A. Marchand, *Byron's Letters and Journals* (London, 1974) ii.34.
4. *Childe Harold's Pilgrimage*, ii, 75.
5. Ibid., ii, 84.
6. *The Giaour.*
7. *Bride of Abydos*, i, i.
8. Quoted from Richard Clogg (ed.) *The Movement for Greek Independence* (London, 1976) p. 59.
9. *Don Juan*, vi, 41.
10. Ibid., iji, after 86.
11. Count Gamba, *A Narrative of Lord Byron's Last Journey to Greece*, (London, 1825) p. 125.
12. Quoted by Fletcher 'Byron in Nineteenth-century Greek Literature' in R. Clogg (ed.) *The Struggle for Greek Independence* (London, 1973).
13. Ibid.

10 Greece Old and New

Tom Winnifrith

It is not the intention of this collection of essays to cover the vast stretch of time which separates the world of Odysseus from the world of Odysseus Elytis. Except for Professor Forrest's stimulating introduction the history of Greece in the last forty years does not receive a great deal of attention. There has been no shortage of other books on modern Greek history, although some of the subjects covered, like the Civil War and the years of the Junta, are still controversial. The story of Classical Greece is relevant to these years. The determination of the English and the Greeks to help each other in checking the Nazis seemed both in England and Greece to be an echo of Leonidas and Themistocles. In the Resistance Classical dons from England fought side by side with Greek heroes who could have been fighting in the *Iliad*. The tragedy of the Civil War divided brother from brother with the stark inevitability of an Aeschylean tragedy. It was appropriate that a communist leader should call himself Ares after the god of war, and the savage treatment of his dead body was as grim as anything we find in Homer.

But it is a mistake to look at Modern Greek history simply through Ancient Greek spectacles. Mr St Clair's and Dr Cartledge's essays are useful reminders of how very different Greece and Greeks had become in the two millennia which followed the Classical period. As well as Byron, Greeks like Solomos and Rhigis Pheraios played their part in the nineteenth-century revival which led to a reawakening among the Greeks themselves of an interest in their illustrious past. Sometimes this revival took an absurd form, especially in the attempts to reimpose an artificial language based on Ancient Greek in place of the normal language of the Greek people. There was a brief attempt under the Junta to teach the artificial Katharevousa in schools instead of the more natural demotic, but demotic would seem to have won the day, although the educationally disastrous effects of the language question are still felt, and are a warning against mixing old Greek wine in new Greek bottles.

Of the many visitors to Greece each year there are some who are interested in no Greek before Aristotle Onassis, and this book is not intended for this kind of tourist. There are others who have not much knowledge of or interest in any Greeks after Aristotle, and this book is intended both to stimulate their interest and to repair the gaps in their knowledge. The rich and varied history of Byzantium tends, as Professor Browning has shown, either to be ignored or to be despised by most English readers. At best we know something of Byzantium through Gibbon, the title of whose *Decline and Fall of the Roman Empire* gives the game away, or through western accounts of the Crusades, picturing the Byzantines as treacherous or unreliable allies. The Fourth Crusade, which ruined Byzantium, is hardly an advertisement for western fair dealing and the amazement of the rough Crusaders at the rich civilisation they found is hardly an advertisement for western culture, but we hear less of this in English history books than the perfidy of Alexios Komnenos and the nobility of Richard Coeur de Lion. At worst we know nothing at all about the Byzantine Empire, full though it is of heroic Achilles-like figures such as Basil the Bulgar Slayer, or crafty Odysseus-like figures such as Alexios Komnenos or tragic Oedipus-like figures like Manuel Palaiologos. Alternatively, following a long tradition of Classical scholarship we despise Byzantine writers for allowing ἀπό to be followed by the accusative, simultaneously and paradoxically condemning them for slavish imitations of Classical models, and ignoring their contribution to preserving Classical texts.

Admittedly Byzantine writers are inferior to their Classical predecessors. The *Epic of Digenis Akritas* is no *Iliad*, and Anna Komnena cannot be compared to Thucydides as a historian. Byzantine art and architecture are in their own way as impressive as, and better preserved than, anything the Classical Age can produce, but it is Classical literature which makes Classical history something uniquely worth studying, and here Byzantium cannot really compete. Yet Byzantine history is worth studying for its own sake, although it is difficult. In Greek and Roman history of the Classical period we have just about the right amount of source material for generations of scholars to work over, and generations of students to flex their muscles on before becoming Treasury mandarins like Mr St Clair. In Byzantine history the sources are inconveniently too few or too many, not enough archaeological work has been done, and basic texts are either inaccessible, or badly edited, or in inconvenient foreign languages like Coptic or Armenian. Perhaps these difficulties should be a challenge to the aspiring research student. Since Classical history has been so exhaustively treated, there is surely more incentive to do work in an area where so much still has to be done.

Certainly Byzantine history, and for that matter Ottoman history, where even less work has been done, are important. Some of the recent interests in Byzantine history has been sparked off by a feeling that unlike our grandfathers we are not living in the age of Pericles but in the age of Manuel Palaiologos, an age of desperate short term measures of expediency with disaster waiting round the corner. This Thucydidean view of history may appear too idealistic to some, but on a more practical level a knowledge of Byzantine history is still essential to an understanding of Balkan politics which were the cause of the First World War and played an important part in the Second. Disputes between various Balkan states are still referred back to various episodes in Byzantine history, and regrettably for the objective historian the reverse is also true. Hence there is all the more need for those trained in an objective discipline such as Greats at Oxford, and without any axe to grind, to turn their attention to Byzantine history.

Nor must we forget the noble part played by successive Byzantine emperors in resisting invasions from north and east. Generations of schoolchildren are brought up to feel that if the Greeks had lost the battle of Salamis, life in Europe would have been infinitely worse and infinitely poorer. The ifs of history are imponderable, and it would not necessarily have been the case that if Salamis had been lost we would all be studying Persian under some Ayatollah Khomeini dictatorship instead of the Classics in a Western democracy. It is indeed much more probable that if the Byzantine empire had not held out against Avar, Slav, Arab and Turk so long and so successfully until the Western nations were ready to receive their inheritance, the history of Europe would have been infinitely poorer. The Byzantine archaising habit of referring to invaders from the north as Scythians and invaders from the east as Persians, infuriating and misleading as it is for the student of ethnology, showed that medieval Greeks as much as Lord Byron saw themselves as descendants of the heroes of the Persian war.

Another apparently infuriating habit of Byzantine historians is that they call themselves not Greeks, but Romans. But this habit is not all that misleading. Even today Greeks occasionally call their language Romaic. The Byzantine empire saw itself as the descendant of the Roman Empire, as indeed it was even after the seventh century, when a knowledge of Latin, apart from a few ceremonial phrases, rapidly died out. In order to understand the whole network of elaborate bureaucracy surrounding the figure of the Emperor one has to have some knowledge of Roman history since bureaucracy and one man rule seem so alien to the Classical Greek spirit. This is yet one more incentive to the Greatsman to turn to Byzantine history rather than the Treasury, although as well as understanding Greek history and Roman history the potential Byzantine scholar must also understand Greek Orthodox Christianity, a study of which is regrettably not included in this volume, although Professors Browning and Bryer refer to it. Greek Orthodoxy is something very different from the religion of the Classical Greeks, and perhaps should not be discussed in a volume entitled *Greece Old and New*. It is surely significant as well as confusing that in early Byzantine writers the term Hellene should be synonymous with pagan.

Another problem for students of Byzantine history is that the Byzantine Empire, like the Roman Empire, was a multi-national state. In Modern Greece even the tiny minorities that speak languages other than Greek now feel themselves Greeks, although this was not always the case fifty years ago. In ancient Greece those who did not speak Greek were counted as barbarians, and perhaps this simple attitude has coloured Modern Greek feeling. But it would have been different in medieval times, when, although Greek was the language of culture, the Church and administration, other languages and nationalities were clearly tolerated. No fewer than three of the essays in this volume deal with the ethnological problems of the Byzantine period, together with their links with Classical and modern problems. It is true that after treating of Greeks and Vlachs, Greeks and Albanians, and Greeks and Turks we rather cautiously stayed away from the most controversial problem of Greeks and Slavs.

Ever since Fallmerayer propounded the thesis that the Modern Greeks had not a drop of the blood of the Ancient Greeks in their veins much ink has been spilt in trying to prove or disprove the purity of the Greek race. This controversy which predates the foundation of the Greek state by two years seems rather a sterile one, and after a hundred and fifty years some kind of resolution does seem possible. Clearly the Slavs penetrated what is now Greece in large numbers during the seventh century, although in the absence of any reliable literary or archaeological evidence it is difficult to establish the extent or the duration of this penetration. Clearly also Greek survived to such an extent that the Slavs in Greece were eventually assimilated, and became Greek-speakers imbued with Greek culture, although, as Professor Bryer has shown, it took the Turkish conquest to sharpen the Greeks' consciousness of their own national identity. If many Greeks have Slav blood in their veins, many Turks must also have Greek blood. Doctrines of racial purity are unpopular, and rightly so in view of the excesses of some of their exponents, but they also do not make sense in the Balkan peninsula. Yet there is nothing wrong in being both aware of and proud of the Greeks' unique cultural and linguistic heritage.

The greatest monument to this heritage is Homer. An epic strain is very strongly present throughout medieval and modern Greek literature, and, whereas it is possible, except at the University of Warwick, to study epics such as Milton's without a prior study of Homer, this is virtually impossible in the case of writers such as Kazantzakis and Elytis. The epics of Digenis Akritas and Erotokritos depend less upon Homer, and it can be argued that it is misleading to call these poems epics. It could also be argued that western epics following Vergil preserve the form of Homer, writing as Byron put it facetiously,

> twelve books . . . after the style of Vergil and of Homer,
> so that my name of Epic is no misnomer,

but abandon or alter Homer's themes. Greek poets on the other hand stick closer to the matter of Homer, but each poet adopts his own manner. There are epic touches in Solomos and Palamas and in the great body of Greek folk songs which look on life and on death with the same clear, but not cold, eye as Homer. Homeric scholarship, whether of the old-fashioned analytical school, or the new formulaic school, has tended to concentrate not enough on what Homer is saying, and too much on the way he says it, and modern Greek poetry is as much of a corrective to this approach as Professor Willcock's discriminating essay. There is however a great deal that students of epic could learn from a study of Greek poetry, and vice versa.

In the case of drama the influence of the Classics has been perhaps too strong for modern Greek dramatists. In a land where the plays of Aeschylus, Sophocles, Euripides and Aristophanes, enacted in ancient theatres but using Modern Greek, attract huge audiences, a modern dramatist must feel himself a trifle cramped. The English schoolboy or student has the choice of studying Greek drama in the original, or in a number of not very felicitous translations; his Greek equivalent has a via media, although perhaps the very excellence of these semi-translations has prevented enough study of Ancient Greek drama or enough writing of modern drama.

Poets, however, have proliferated. Seferis' phrase 'the ancient monuments and contemporary sorrow', τ'αρχαια μνημεια και τη συγχρονη θλιψη, shows that Modern Greek poets, however modern, difficult or surrealistic, have a ready shared frame of reference in the Greek landscape and the history of Ancient Greece which their English equivalents lack. It is unfortunate that so much of modern Greek poetry, if not lost in translation, is lost through not being translated, and we are very fortunate in this volume to have a poem of Yannis Ritsos translated by Nikos Stangos. This poem and its translator show better and more briefly than this postscript how Modern Greek has both preserved and renewed its Classical heritage.

11 Septeria and Daphnephoria

Nikos Stangos (translated from *Repetitions* by Yannis Ritsos)

We said: this year we are going to stay put. Enough of this. What silly expeditions.
Man's only wisdom is to be alone. So why rush now
Out into the night with torches, stumbling over stones, without even knowing
The meaning of such pointless symbols — the building of the wooden shed,
The arcane procession headed by a youth, the arrow transfixed in the door,
And setting fire then to the shed, everyone running towards Tempe
Without turning to look back; and turning back again after the sacrifices
Loaded with laurel branches. The same things over and over again,
Every nine years (perhaps so that we can forget in the meantime — and we do forget). Ah, no!
This time we are not going to budge — that is what we said. But when
The distant drum was heard and the torch-bearers noiselessly passed the house,
We couldn't, once again, resist; we ran into the street, jostling in the crowd,
We took part in the burning, the running, the sacrifices, and we returned

Down the Pythian road towards Delphi, after midnight, carrying
Bunches and bunches of laurels, although (for years now) there
  was no one to crown —
And we felt sad but also proud that no one knew and that everyone
Still reckons us to be one one them — . The shed still smouldered at
  day-break. Returning home
We looked at the sky, clear, milky, azure, rosy; we looked, on the
  ground,
At little, trampled paper flags, at a child's sandals, at a handker-
  chief with sperm;
We looked on calmly, ecstatically, with vague politeness and vague
  nausea,
Pleasantly tired and dazed by the long sleeplessness,
Like actors, their make-up removed, at the end of a beautiful per-
  formance, who walk away retaining
In their sleepy ears the vain roar of applause and also a certain
Irritation, the way a little bit of glue remains still on their chins
  from the venerable beard
Of Oedipus or of Prometheus, which they had worn again tonight.

Index